I'm convinced that the Bible is somehow powerfully si
complex. Like a diamond viewed from different angle
confronts my heart in fresh ways. This Bible-study ser
perspectives and gives its participants a refreshing opportunity to admire the
character of God and be transformed by the truth of his Word. Our souls need
to meander through the minutiae and metanarrative of the Bible, and the
Storyline Bible Studies help us do both.

> KYLE IDLEMAN, senior pastor of Southeast Christian Church and bestselling author of *Not a Fan* and *One at a Time*

If you are longing for a breath of fresh air in your spiritual life, this study is
for you. Kat Armstrong brings to life both familiar and less familiar Bible
stories in such an engaging way that you can't help but see how the God of
the past is also working and moving in your present. Through the captivating
truths revealed in this series, you will discover more about God's faithfulness,
be equipped to move past fear and disappointment, and be empowered to be
who you were created to be. If your faith has felt mundane or routine, these
words will be a refreshing balm to your soul and a guide to go deeper in your
relationship with God.

> HOSANNA WONG, international speaker and bestselling author of *How (Not) to Save the World: The Truth about Revealing God's Love to the People Right Next to You*

We are watching a new wave of Bible studies that care about the Bible's big
story, from Genesis to Revelation; that plunge Bible readers into the depths
of human despair and show them the glories of the Kingdom God plans
for creation; and that invite readers to participate in that story in all its
dimensions—in the mountains and the valleys. Anyone who ponders these
Bible studies will come to terms not only with the storyline of the Bible but
also with where each of us fits in God's grand narrative. I heartily commend
Kat's **Storyline Bible Studies**.

> REV. CANON DR. SCOT McKNIGHT, professor of New Testament at Northern Seminary

Kat Armstrong is an able trail guide with contagious enthusiasm! In this series, she'll take you hiking through Scripture to experience mountains and valleys, sticks and stones, sinners and saints. If you are relatively new to the Bible or are struggling to see how it all fits together, your trek with Kat will be well worth it. You might even decide that hiking through the Bible is your new hobby.

CARMEN JOY IMES, associate professor of Old Testament at Biola University and author of *Bearing God's Name: Why Sinai Still Matters*

Kat Armstrong takes you into the heart of Scripture so that Scripture can grow in your heart. The **Storyline Bible Studies** have everything: the overarching story of God's redemption, the individual biblical story's historical context, and the text's interpretation that connects with today's realities. Armstrong asks insightful questions that make the Bible come alive and draws authentically on her own faith journey so that readers might deepen their relationship with Jesus. Beautifully written and accessible, the **Storyline Bible Studies** are a wonderful resource for individual or group study.

LYNN H. COHICK, PhD, provost and dean of academic affairs at Northern Seminary

Christians affirm that the Bible is God's Word and provides God's life-giving instruction and encouragement. But what good is such an authoritative and valuable text if God's people don't engage it to find the help the Scriptures provide? Here's where Kat Armstrong's studies shine. In each volume, she presents Bible study as a journey through Scripture that can be transformational. In the process, she enables readers to see the overarching storyline of the Bible and to find their place in that story. In addition, Armstrong reinforces the essential steps that make Bible study life-giving for people seeking to grow in their faith. Whether for individuals, for small groups, or as part of a church curriculum, these studies are ideally suited to draw students into a fresh and invigorating engagement with God's Word.

WILLIAM W. KLEIN, PhD, professor emeritus of New Testament interpretation and author of *Handbook for Personal Bible Study: Enriching Your Experience with God's Word*

Kat has done two things that I love. She's taken something that is familiar and presented it in a fresh way that is understandable by all, balancing the profound with accessibility. And her trustworthy and constant approach to Bible study equips the participant to emerge from this study with the ability to keep studying and growing more.

MARTY SOLOMON, creator and executive producer of *The BEMA Podcast*

You are in for an adventure. In this series, Kat pulls back the curtain to reveal how intentionally God has woven together seemingly disconnected moments in the collective Bible story. Her delivery is both brilliant and approachable. She will invite you to be a curious sleuth as you navigate familiar passages of Scripture, discovering things you'd never seen before. I promise you will never read the living Word the same again.

JENN JETT BARRETT, founder and visionary of The Well Summit

Kat has done it again! The same wisdom, depth, humility, and authenticity that we have come to expect from her previous work is on full display here in her new **Storyline Bible Study** series. Kat is the perfect guide through these important themes and through the story of Scripture: gentle and generous on the one hand, capable and clear on the other. She is a gifted communicator and teacher of God's Word. The format of these studies is helpful too—perfect pacing, just the right amount of new information at each turn, with plenty of space for writing and prayerful reflection as you go and some great resources for further study. I love learning from Kat, and I'm sure you will too. Grab a few friends from your church or neighborhood and dig into these incredible resources together to find your imagination awakened and your faith strengthened.

DAN LOWERY, president of Pillar Seminary

Kat Armstrong possesses something I deeply admire: a sincere and abiding respect for the Bible. Her tenaciousness to know more about her beloved Christ, her commitment to truth telling, and her desire to dig until she mines the deepest gold for her Bible-study readers makes her one of my favorite Bible teachers. I find few that match her scriptural attentiveness and even fewer that embody her humble spirit. This project is stunning, like the rest of her work.

LISA WHITTLE, bestselling author of *Jesus over Everything: Uncomplicating the Daily Struggle to Put Jesus First*, Bible teacher, and podcast host

SINNERS

EXPERIENCING JESUS' COMPASSION
IN THE MIDDLE OF YOUR SIN, STRUGGLES, AND SHAME

KAT ARMSTRONG

A NavPress resource published in alliance
with Tyndale House Publishers

NavPress is the publishing ministry of The Navigators, an international Christian organization and leader in personal spiritual development. NavPress is committed to helping people grow spiritually and enjoy lives of meaning and hope through personal and group resources that are biblically rooted, culturally relevant, and highly practical.

For more information, visit NavPress.com.

Sinners: Experiencing Jesus' Compassion in the Middle of Your Sin, Struggles, and Shame

Copyright © 2023 by Kat Armstrong. All rights reserved.

A NavPress resource published in alliance with Tyndale House Publishers

NavPress and the NavPress logo are registered trademarks of NavPress, The Navigators, Colorado Springs, CO. *Tyndale* is a registered trademark of Tyndale House Ministries. Absence of ® in connection with marks of NavPress or other parties does not indicate an absence of registration of those marks.

The Team:
David Zimmerman, Publisher; Caitlyn Carlson, Acquisitions Editor; Elizabeth Schroll, Copy Editor; Olivia Eldredge, Operations Manager; Julie Chen, Designer; Sarah K. Johnson and Ian K. Smith, Proofreaders

Cover illustration by Lindsey Bergsma. Copyright © 2023 by NavPress/The Navigators. All rights reserved.

Author photo by Judy Rodriguez, copyright © 2021. All rights reserved.

Author is represented by Jana Burson of The Christopher Ferebee Agency, christopherferebee.com

Unless otherwise indicated, all Scripture quotations are taken from the Christian Standard Bible,® copyright © 2017 by Holman Bible Publishers. Used by permission. Christian Standard Bible® and CSB® are federally registered trademarks of Holman Bible Publishers. Scripture quotations marked NRSV are taken from the New Revised Standard Version Bible, copyright © 1989 National Council of the Churches of Christ in the United States of America. Used by permission. All rights reserved worldwide.

Some of the anecdotal illustrations in this book are true to life and are included with the permission of the persons involved. All other illustrations are composites of real situations, and any resemblance to people living or dead is purely coincidental.

For information about special discounts for bulk purchases, please contact Tyndale House Publishers at csresponse@tyndale.com, or call 1-855-277-9400.

ISBN 978-1-64158-596-5

Printed in the United States of America

29	28	27	26	25	24	23
7	6	5	4	3	2	1

For my dad, Ronald K. Obenhaus.
I think you would have loved this.

Contents

A Message from Kat

I WROTE *SINNERS* when I was depressed and anxious. In a matter of weeks, I lived through

- the five-year anniversary of my father's death,
- significant church hurt,
- a two-hundred-page report on sexual abuse in one of the largest Christian denominations, and
- the news of a mass shooting at an elementary school in Uvalde, Texas.

Every day I woke up to more news that evil abounds, and all I could say was, *I am not okay. Christ, have mercy.*

What lifted my spirits? Reading about Jesus' compassion toward sinners. In the chaos and pain and devastation of this world, Jesus is our rescue plan. He came to save sinners like me and you.

As I searched the Scriptures for encouragement, what held my attention and brought peace to my soul was Jesus' tenderheartedness, compassion, and mercy toward the unlikely "sinners" who expressed great faith.

Righteous sinners are all over the New Testament. So much so that I suggest that they are a character archetype in the Scriptures, a literary pattern in the Bible. This pattern highlights God's compassion and kindness for all and emphasizes the beautiful expressions of faith from people burdened with sin, struggles, and shame.

These memorable people will be the focus of our study together, and I'm confident that anyone seeking peace for their soul, anyone struggling to abide in this world, anyone defeated by circumstance will be encouraged by God's rescue plan: Jesus came to save sinners like us.

I'm praying that your time studying righteous sinners in the Bible is an awe-inspiring catalyst to engage and experience God's truth—that you would marvel at the artistry of God's storytelling. And that the righteous sinners in the Bible will help you stay gentle and tender in a world so hardened and broken.

Love,

Kat

The Storyline of Scripture

YOUR DECISION TO STUDY THE BIBLE for the next few weeks is no accident—God has brought you here, to this moment. And I don't want to take it for granted. Here, at the beginning, I want to invite you into the most important step you can take, the one that brings the whole of the Bible alive in extraordinary ways: a relationship with Jesus.

The Bible is a collection of divinely inspired manuscripts written over fifteen hundred years by at least forty different authors. Together, the manuscripts make up tens of thousands of verses, sixty-six books, and two testaments. Point being: It's a lot of content.

But the Bible is really just one big story: God's story of redemption. From Genesis to Revelation the Bible includes narratives, songs, poems, wisdom literature, letters, and even apocalyptic prophecies. Yet everything we read in God's Word helps us understand God's love and his plan to be in a relationship with us.

If you hear nothing else, hear this: God loves you.

It's easy to get lost in the vast amount of information in the Bible, so we're going to explore the storyline of Scripture in four parts. And as you locate your experience in the story of the Bible, I hope the story of redemption becomes your own.

PART 1: GOD MADE SOMETHING GOOD.

The big story—God's story of redemption—started in a garden. When God launched his project for humanity, he purposed all of us—his image bearers—to flourish and co-create with him. In the beginning there was peace, beauty, order, and abundant life. The soil was good. Life was good. We rarely hear this part of our story, but it doesn't make it less true. God created something good—and that includes you.

PART 2: WE MESSED IT UP.

If you've ever thought, *This isn't how it's supposed to be*, you're right. It's not. We messed up God's good world. Do you ever feel like you've won gold medals in messing things up? Me too. All humanity shares in that brokenness. We are imperfect. The people we love are imperfect. Our systems are jacked, and our world is broken. And that's on us. We made the mess, and we literally can't help ourselves. We need to be rescued from our circumstances, the systems in which we live, and ourselves.

PART 3: JESUS MAKES IT RIGHT.

The good news is that God can clean up all our messes, and he does so through the life, death, and resurrection of Jesus Christ. No one denies that Jesus lived and died. That's just history. It's the empty tomb and the hundreds of eyewitnesses who saw Jesus after his death that make us scratch our heads. Because science can only prove something that is repeatable, we are dependent upon the eyewitness testimonies of Jesus' resurrection for this once-in-history moment. If Jesus rose from the dead—and I believe he did—Jesus is exactly who he said he was, and he accomplished exactly what had been predicted for thousands of years. He restored us. Jesus made *it*, all of it, right. He can forgive your sins and connect you to the holy God through his life, death, and resurrection.

PART 4: ONE DAY, GOD WILL MAKE ALL THINGS NEW.

The best news is that this is not as good as it gets. A day is coming when Christ will return. He's coming back to re-create our world: a place with no tears, no pain, no suffering, no brokenness, no helplessness—just love. God will make all things new. In the meantime, God invites you to step into his storyline, to join him in his work of restoring all things. Rescued restorers live with purpose and on mission: not a life devoid of hardship, but one filled with enduring hope.

RESPONDING TO GOD'S STORYLINE

If the storyline of Scripture feels like a lightbulb turning on in your soul, that, my friend, is the one true, living God, who eternally exists as Father, Son, and Holy Spirit. God is inviting you into a relationship with him to have your sins forgiven and secure a place in his presence forever. When you locate your story within God's story of redemption, you begin a lifelong relationship with God that brings meaning, hope, and restoration to your life.

Take a moment now to begin a relationship with Christ:

God, I believe the story of the Bible, that Jesus is Lord and you raised him from the dead to forgive my sins and make our relationship possible. Your storyline is now my story. I want to learn how to love you and share your love with others. Amen.

If you confess with your lips that Jesus is Lord and believe in your heart that God raised him from the dead, you will be saved.

ROMANS 10:9, NRSV

How to Use This Bible Study

THE **STORYLINE BIBLE STUDIES** are versatile and can be used for

- individual study (self-paced),
- small groups (five- or ten-lesson curriculum), or
- church ministry (semester-long curriculum).

INDIVIDUAL STUDY

Each lesson in the *Sinners* Bible study is divided into four fifteen- to twenty-minute parts (sixty to eighty minutes of individual study time per lesson). You can work through the material one part at a time over a few different days or all in one sitting. Either way, this study will be like anything good in your life: What you put in, you get out. Each of the four parts of each lesson will help you practice Bible-study methods.

SMALL GROUPS

Working through the *Sinners* Bible study with a group could be a catalyst for life change. Although the Holy Spirit can teach you truth when you read the Bible on your own, I want to encourage you to gather a small group together to work through this study for these reasons:

- God himself is in communion as one essence and three persons: Father, Son, and Holy Spirit.
- Interconnected, interdependent relationships are hallmarks of the Christian faith life.
- When we collaborate with each other in Bible study, we have access to the viewpoints of our brothers and sisters in Christ, which enrich our understanding of the truth.

For this Bible study, every small-group member will need a copy of the *Sinners* study guide. In addition, I've created a free downloadable small-group guide that includes

- discussion questions for each lesson,
- Scripture readings, and
- prayer prompts.

Whether you've been a discussion leader for decades or just volunteered to lead a group for the first time, you'll find the resources you need to create a loving atmosphere for men and women to grow in Christlikeness. You can download the small-group guide using this QR code.

CHURCH MINISTRY

Church and ministry leaders: Your work is sacred. I know that planning and leading through a semester of ministry can be both challenging and rewarding. That's why every **Storyline Bible Study** is written so that you can build modular semesters of ministry. The *Sinners* Bible study is designed to complement the

Saints Bible study. Together, *Sinners* and *Saints* can support a whole semester of ministry seamlessly, inviting the people you lead into God's Word and making your life simpler.

To further equip church and ministry leaders, I've created *The Leader's Guide*, a free digital resource. You can download *The Leader's Guide* using this QR code.

The Leader's Guide offers these resources:

+ a sample ministry calendar for a ten-plus-lesson semester of ministry,
+ small-group discussion questions for each lesson,
+ Scripture readings for each lesson,
+ prayer prompts for each lesson,
+ five teaching topics for messages that could be taught in large-group settings, and
+ resources for deeper study.

SPECIAL FEATURES

However you decide to utilize the *Sinners* Bible study, whether for individual, self-paced devotional time; as a small-group curriculum; or for semester-long church ministry, you'll notice several stand-out features unique to the **Storyline Bible Studies**:

+ gospel presentation at the beginning of each Bible study;
+ full Scripture passages included in the study so that you can mark up the text and keep your notes in one place;
+ insights from diverse scholars, authors, and Bible teachers;
+ an emphasis on close readings of large portions of Scripture;
+ following one theme instead of focusing on one verse or passage;
+ Christological narrative theology without a lot of church-y words; and
+ retrospective or imaginative readings of the Bible to help Christians follow the storyline of Scripture.

You may have studied the Bible by book, topic, or passage before; all those approaches are enriching ways to read the Word of God. The **Storyline Bible Studies** follow a literary thread to deepen your appreciation for God's master plan of redemption and develop your skill in connecting the Old Testament to the New.

THE SINNERS STORYLINE

"IS ANAKIN SKYWALKER one of the good guys?"

My son, Caleb, has started asking some curious questions about Star Wars—his favorite movie series. Although he doesn't yet have the language to articulate the themes he's picking up on, Caleb can easily identify basic character types.

Television programming for grade-school kids often reduces characters into two categories: good and bad. But as soon as Caleb started enjoying more complex stories, he had trouble identifying the good guys and the bad guys. Sometimes it felt as though characters were a mix of both.

Caleb is a long way off from literature classes where he'll learn about more nuanced character archetypes. But he's intuitively learning that characters like Boromir from The Lord of the Rings and Anakin Skywalker from Star Wars are tragic hero types. Flawed leaders. Good guys who do bad things. And you and I know that the complex characters in our favorite stories more closely resemble real-life people.

The Bible is a literary masterpiece for infinite reasons, and one way God's artistic brilliance unfolds is through his archetypes. We see throughout the Scriptures that God is not only comfortable preserving the confusing actions of complex characters but also purposeful in layering their character development in order to teach us timeless truths.

In *Sinners*, we're going to explore one of these startling and powerful truths: that some of the bad guys repent faster than the good ones.

In a bout of depression, I found great comfort zeroing in on the "sinful" characters in the New Testament who exhibited great faith in Christ. In some cases, these people were considered sinful because of their behaviors, their lifestyles, their titles, or their ethnic backgrounds. Often, the people who experienced Jesus' compassion most powerfully were struggling with sin and shame.

You and I are going to discover together God's tender compassion for *anyone*—regardless of their social status, regardless of their past, regardless of their labels. And we are going to notice the counterintuitive ways "sinful" people responded to Jesus in righteous acts of faith. You'll start to see a theme unfold: The people considered sinful often acted with greater faith than the most religious people of Jesus' day.

Palestinian Judaism generally followed its scriptural heritage by warning of conduct that was deemed "sinful" and persons who were regarded as "sinners." Yet these were not simply moral terms for violators of God's law. What was regarded as "sin" and who was a "sinner" were matters of legal dispute among Jewish leaders. In many cases, "sin" and "sinner" were freighted terms within Jewish sectarianism and were deployed in order to denounce or exclude persons for behavior that did not meet the perceived norms of certain Jewish factions.[1]

Michael F. Bird, "Sin, Sinner," in *Dictionary of Jesus and the Gospels*

According to Jesus, it is the restoration of sinners through repentance, rather than the exclusion of sinners from communal life, that is God's intended purpose for sinners.[2]

Michael F. Bird, "Sin, Sinner," in *Dictionary of Jesus and the Gospels*

Every person we survey in this Bible study is deeply embedded in an ancient, symbol-driven world where the characters in a story don't just exist—they also represent concepts larger than the person themselves. Sometimes God repurposes a character archetype to emphasize biblical themes.

The *Sinners* Bible study will guide you through five Bible stories in which a person who is considered sinful by society acts righteously and with great faith. The presence of these people in the Scriptures is a key element in the story, embodying truths about God.

In *Sinners*, we're going to explore

- *Matthew 9*: the disciple and former tax collector named Matthew who leaves his tollbooth to follow Jesus and whose faith confuses the religious;
- *Luke 7*: the Roman centurion who advocates for his sick servant and whose faith saves the servant's life;
- *Luke 7*: the sinful woman who anoints Jesus with the perfume from her alabaster jar and whose faith saves her;
- *Matthew 15*: the Canaanite mom who begs Jesus to heal her demon-possessed daughter and whose faith leads to her daughter's healing; and
- *John 4*: the Samaritan woman at the well who is approached by Jesus and whose faith starts revival in her town.

We're going to do this by looking at each righteous sinner through four different lenses:

- **PART 1: CONTEXT.** Do you ever feel dropped into a Bible story disoriented? Part 1 will introduce you to the character you're going to study and help you study their story in its scriptural context. Getting your bearings before you read will enable you to answer the question *What am I about to read?*

- **PART 2: SEEING.** Do you ever read on autopilot? I do too. Sometimes I finish reading without a clue as to what just happened. A better way to read the Bible is to practice thoughtful, close reading of Scripture to absorb the message God is offering to us. That's why part 2 includes close Scripture reading and observation questions to empower you to answer the question *What is the story saying?*

- **PART 3: UNDERSTANDING.** If you've ever scratched your head after reading your Bible, part 3 will give you the tools to understand the author's intended meaning both for the original audience and for you. Plus you'll practice connecting the Old and New Testaments to get a fuller picture of God's unchanging grace. Part 3 will enable you to answer the question *What does it mean?*

- **PART 4: RESPONDING.** The purpose of Bible study is to help you become more Christlike; that's why part 4 will include journaling space for your reflection on and responses to the content and a blank checklist for actionable next steps. You'll be able to process what you're learning so that you can live out the concepts and pursue Christlikeness. Part 4 will enable you to answer the questions *What truths is this passage teaching?* and *How do I apply this to my life?*

One of my prayers for you, as a curious Bible reader, is that our journey through this study will help you cultivate a biblical imagination so that you're able to make connections throughout the whole storyline of the Bible. In each lesson, I'll do my best to include a few verses from different places in the Bible that are connected to our sinner's story. In the course of this study, we'll see the way God shows up for righteous sinners throughout his Word—and get a glimpse of how he might show up in our lives today.

God's Word is so wonderful, I hardly know how to contain my excitement. Feel free to geek out with me; let your geek flag fly high, my friends. When we can see how interrelated all the parts of Scripture are to each other, we'll find our affection for God stirred as we see his artistic brilliance unfold.

LEAVING YOUR SECURITY
BEHIND TO FOLLOW JESUS

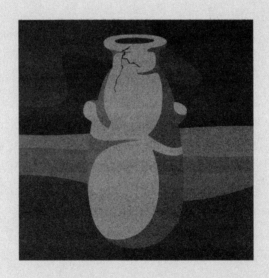

THE TAX COLLECTOR:
THE FAITH OF THE DISCIPLE WHO LEAVES HIS TOLLBOOTH

SCRIPTURE: MATTHEW 9

PART 1

CONTEXT

Before you begin your study, we will start with the context of the story we are about to read together: the setting, both cultural and historical; the people involved; and where our passage fits in the larger setting of Scripture. All these things help us make sense of what we're reading. Understanding the context of a Bible story is fundamental to reading Scripture well. Getting your bearings before you read will enable you to answer the question *What am I about to read?*

MY HUSBAND, AARON, sold cars right out of college and into our early years of marriage. We don't miss the late nights on the car lot or the ups and downs of commission-based living, but we sure do miss the demo cars—the nicest rides of our lives.

Whenever we told our friends and family what we were up to, we'd get a lot of confused looks in response to Aaron's profession. Sometimes we could tell that people were trying to fix their faces so their disapproval wouldn't show. But of all the reactions, one stands out the most. I was working at a marketing firm when a client—a professor—asked me more about myself. I shared that I was a new seminary student and that my husband also had plans to start seminary, which of course led to the question of what Aaron was doing in the meantime. I thought the professor was going to slide out of his chair, melt into the ground, and lose consciousness at my answer. He was mortified. And he told me why: Car sales-men are "slick."

The car industry looks different twenty years later, but people often still stereo-type people in the car-sales business as untrustworthy. We might feel the same way about politicians and attorneys. And yes, like all professions, these career paths could use some reforms. I don't want to diminish those issues. But sometimes a person's job title overshadows their humanness. Instead of a job being what someone does, the caricature of their position defines who they are.

In the first century, tax collectors fell prey to dehumanizing stereotypes too. The New Testament offers plenty of reasons why this was the case:

- A tax collector was "someone responsible for collecting taxes and tolls on behalf of the Roman government."[1]
- "Tax collectors earned a profit by demanding a higher tax from the people than they had prepaid to the Roman government. This system led to widespread greed and corruption. The tax-collecting profession was saturated with unscrupulous people who overtaxed others to maximize their personal gain."[2]
- "Since the Jews considered themselves victims of Roman oppression, Jewish tax collectors who overtaxed their fellow countrymen were especially despised. Jews viewed such favor for Rome as betrayal and equal to treason against God. Rabbinic sources consistently align Jewish tax collectors with robbers."[3]

Governments have a right to collect taxes, but those who collect them have often been unpopular, not least because they seem to have demanded more than they were entitled to. Jesus Christ welcomed such people, as he did other sinners, and many repented as a result of his affirming attitude.[4]

Martin H. Manser et al., *The Complete Topical Guide to the Bible*

Here are some facts about tax collecting:

- "Romans taxed just about every commodity imaginable."[5]

- "The Jews were also suffering under a system of double-taxation . . . , as they had to pay all of the religious taxes as prescribed by the law (Exod 30:12-16; Matt 17:24-27) as well as the Roman taxes."[6]

- "It has been estimated that a direct sales tax on all produce in Israel may have been as high as 12.5 percent."[7]

- "Furthermore, there is some evidence that the Romans exacted an additional tax from each Jewish household. . . . When one adds to this the various custom taxes required for transporting goods from one region to another, the annual tax burden of the Jews may have been as high as 40 percent of one's total income."[8]

- "The Jews hated paying taxes to the emperor and harbored a deep resentment for those who collected taxes from them."[9]

We might want to make a joke about the IRS right now. Or just mutter, *Taxes—booooo.* Even today, we still feel tempted to lump the profession in with the person. But in Jesus' time, it was far worse: Tax collectors were hated, judged, and considered traitors. They were least liked by the religious elite and considered unclean and unrighteous sinners. That's why Jesus' invitation to Matthew—to join Jesus' inner circle as a disciple—is so astonishing.

In this lesson we are going to study the conversion story of Matthew, the author of the Gospel of Matthew, the first book in the New Testament. Matthew, a tax collector, was minding his business when Jesus approached him, invited Matthew to follow him, and welcomed Matthew as a disciple.

You're about to read the story of a man who likely carried a lot of shame and experienced a lot of rejection because of his job. He was viewed as a sinner by his religious community, and he was absolutely an outsider. But he ended up leaving behind the security of extortion and taxation to start a new life.

If you need a redo, a total overhaul of your life, you're in good company with Matthew. And the rest of us who are eager to experience Jesus' compassion will find an archetypal example of Jesus' love for us and for all sinners. Even the worst of us get invitations to follow Jesus. The only question is whether we will say yes.

1. **PERSONAL CONTEXT: What is going on in your life right now that might impact how you understand this Bible character?**

2. **SPIRITUAL CONTEXT: If you've never studied this Bible story before, what piques your curiosity? If you've studied this passage before, what impressions and insights do you recall?**

SEEING

Seeing the text is vital if we want the heart of the Scripture passage to sink in. We read slowly and intentionally through the text with the context in mind. As we practice close, thoughtful reading of Scripture, we pick up on phrases, implications, and meanings we might otherwise have missed. Part 2 includes close Scripture reading and observation questions to empower you to answer the question *What is the story saying?*

1. Read Matthew 9:9-13 and circle all the verbs in this story.

⁹ As Jesus went on from there, he saw a man named Matthew sitting at the tax office, and he said to him, "Follow me," and he got up and followed him.

¹⁰ While he was reclining at the table in the house, many tax collectors and sinners came to eat with Jesus and his disciples. ¹¹ When the Pharisees saw this, they asked his disciples, "Why does your teacher eat with tax collectors and sinners?"

¹² Now when he heard this, he said, "It is not those who are well who need a doctor, but those who are sick. ¹³ Go and learn what this means: **I desire mercy and not sacrifice. For I didn't come to call the righteous, but sinners.**"

MATTHEW 9:9-13

Right before this scene, Matthew includes a story about Jesus healing a paralyzed man on a stretcher. In fact, all the stories between Jesus' Sermon on the Mount in Matthew 5–7 and this moment are accounts of Jesus healing someone who approached him:

- Jesus healed a man with leprosy (Matthew 8:2-4).
- Jesus healed a centurion's paralyzed servant (Matthew 8:5-13).
- Jesus healed Peter's sick mother-in-law (Matthew 8:14-15).
- Jesus healed many demon-possessed people (Matthew 8:16-17).
- Jesus healed two demon-possessed men in the Gadarenes (Matthew 8:28).
- Jesus healed the paralyzed man on the stretcher (Matthew 9:1-8).

Matthew is making a point. The same Jesus preaching about the Kingdom of God brought heaven to earth through his healing ministry. And Matthew was no exception to this healing. He had no outward ailments, but he needed to heal from shame. It is within this context that Matthew gives us a window into his experience and how he understood Jesus' life, death, and resurrection.

Second, Matthew makes clear an interesting distinction: All the people Jesus healed physically approached Jesus in their pain and desperation . . . but not Matthew. He stands out in the series of stories in Matthew's Gospel. Jesus came *to Matthew*. Do you need to hear that today? As far away as you feel from Christ, he is pursuing you.

As Jesus will explain several times throughout his ministry, he came to heal the sick, give sight to the blind, and set the prisoners free. And he does so by getting close to us. Whether we seek him out or he comes to find us, we will be found. Jesus has compassion on both the initiative takers and the ones who need to be invited. Thank God.

2. According to Matthew 9:9, what was Matthew doing at the tollbooth when Jesus saw him?

3. In what two ways did Matthew respond to Christ's invitation to follow him (Matthew 9:9)?

- ◆

- ◆

When Matthew heard Jesus' call to join his mission, he stood up and moved toward Christ. He stood up not only for Christ—he stood up for himself, perhaps for the first time taking faithful steps to move forward in his life. For too long, he'd settled for advancing the cause of Rome. Not anymore. Matthew left his post to be near his Savior.

Soon enough, Matthew would witness the taxing sacrifice Jesus was willing to make to pay off all our debts. Jesus would offer his own life to save ours. Matthew left the tollbooth with the One who could pay all the tolls and destroy all the booths. Jesus, the only person not taxed by corrupt powers, chose to pay the full and ultimate price for our salvation.

4. Write out what Jesus said in Matthew 9:9 that caused Matthew to leave behind his tollbooth:

❝

❞

Jesus used this phrase, and words like it, many more times in the Gospels. Correspondingly, more people like Matthew left their posts to follow Jesus. Jesus had similar conversations with a man asking about eternal life (Matthew 19:21), the disciple Philip (John 1:43), and Peter (John 21:22).

I looked up every instance of "Follow me" in the New Testament and found several courageous sinners choosing Christ over their insecurities, failures, and pasts. This is a wake-up call for me, and I hope it spurs you forward. No matter what holds you back from running to the arms of your Savior, you can get up and follow Christ.

5. **List anything you imagine Matthew thinking and feeling as he stood up and left his tollbooth:**

-
-
-
-
-

A lot happens between Matthew leaving his tollbooth (Matthew 9:9) and his dinner party with Jesus (Matthew 9:10). Matthew doesn't give us as many details as I would like. I have so many questions!

- Was the dinner party hosted at Matthew's house?
- Did Matthew already have dinner plans with these people, or did he invite them spontaneously?
- Did the guests know Jesus was coming?
- What did the guests think of Jesus' willingness to spend time with society's outcasts?

6. **List who was on the guest list based on Matthew 9:10-12.**

- Jesus
- Matthew
-
-
-
-
-

I have lots of questions about the other tax collectors in attendance too. Were these Matthew's coworkers? Or could they be the tax collectors John the Baptist baptized in Luke 3:12? If these tax collectors had already been baptized and had followed Jesus in his preaching and healing ministry, did Matthew find community with other Christ-following tax collectors?

You likely have an affinity group who supports you in life and faith. Think about the intramural sports teams, clubs, men's and women's ministry groups at church, friend groups that bunch together because of parenting or a hobby. Where would we be without like-minded people encouraging us to keep going?

7. **What are some of the reasons the Pharisees, the religious elite, would have been offended by Jesus' behavior (Matthew 9:11)?**

8. **Write out what Jesus said after hearing the Pharisees criticize his choice of dinner companions (Matthew 9:12).**

"

"

In the next part of our study, we are going to explore Jesus' intended meaning when he told the Pharisees, "I desire mercy and not sacrifice" (Matthew 9:13). Until then, I want to remind you that Jesus considered Matthew one of the sick he had come to heal. Maybe you feel sick to your stomach over your wrongdoings or the wrongdoings of others. Maybe you feel sick to death about the hardships you're facing or the questionable decisions you've made in the past. However you relate to Matthew's "sickness," remember this: Jesus is the healer you need. He tenderly offers you medical and spiritual attention, even when you feel you can't approach him. He invites you to be seen and cared for, and he wants you to come just as you are.

PART 3

UNDERSTANDING

Now that we've finished a close reading of the Scriptures, we're going to spend some time on interpretation: doing our best to understand what God was saying to the original audience and what he's teaching us through the process. But to do so, we need to learn his ways and consider how God's Word would have been understood by the original audience before applying the same truths to our own lives. "Scripture interpretation" may sound a little stuffy, but understanding what God means to communicate to us in the Bible is crucial to enjoying a close relationship with Jesus. Part 3 will enable you to answer the question *What does it mean?*

I'VE ATTENDED MY FAIR SHARE of awkward dinner parties, and I'm sure you have too. Maybe you've hosted two guests who, unbeknownst to you, don't get along. Or you've forgotten a key ingredient in the main dish or burned dinner to a crisp. I have friends who've called someone by the wrong name for the duration of a dinner party only to be mortified later when they've realized the faux pas.

It's easy to laugh off these examples, but I'm convinced this dinner party with

Jesus comes like a physician with a ministry of restoration, reconciliation and repentance for these sinners.[10]

Michael F. Bird, "Sin, Sinner," in *Dictionary of Jesus and the Gospels*

Jesus, his disciples, Matthew, tax collectors, and sinners would have been super awkward—all thanks to an interaction between Jesus and the Pharisees.

The Pharisees asked Jesus' disciples, "Why does your teacher eat with tax collectors and sinners?" (Matthew 9:11), and Jesus responded with three statements:

- "It is not those who are well who need a doctor, but those who are sick" (Matthew 9:12).
- "Go and learn what this means: I desire mercy and not sacrifice" (Matthew 9:13).
- "For I didn't come to call the righteous, but sinners" (Matthew 9:13).

1. What did Jesus mean when he said, "It is not those who are well who need a doctor, but those who are sick"? Who was he calling "sick"?

When Jesus said the Pharisees needed to learn to prioritize mercy over sacrifice, he was quoting an Old Testament verse: Hosea 6:6. "Jesus draws on Hosea to affirm the priority of mercy over sacrifice . . . , and he embodies this priority in his wide welcome of those whom Pharisees and others deem unworthy."[11]

2. Why does God desire mercy over sacrifice?

3. In your own life, what does sacrifice to God look like? What do you sacrifice in the name of following Jesus?

4. When are you most likely to show others mercy? When is it hardest to be merciful?

5. What did Jesus mean when he said, "I didn't come to call the righteous, but sinners"? Who was he calling "righteous" and "sinners"?

The Pharisees' role in society was to be teachers of the Jewish law—and Jesus told them to become students. This is both awkward and funny to me. I can imagine how stunned they might have been at Jesus' zinger, *and* I can picture myself in their place, audacious and ignorant enough to question God. Jesus, the Great Teacher, challenged the Pharisees to learn something new. Based on Matthew 9:12-13, this would require the Pharisees to "go."

We will have to wait until glory to confirm this, but I wonder if their question was sincere. Did they genuinely want to find out the meaning behind Jesus' dinner party with tax collectors and sinners? Or did they ask incredulously? Were they curious or offended? Whatever their reasons, Jesus was patient enough to answer their question and wise enough to invite them to learn for themselves what they thought they already knew.

6. **Describe a time you thought you already knew something in your spiritual life but then developed a deeper or new understanding in your relationship with Jesus.**

Choosing to learn, to relearn, and to unlearn all take courage. That's why Jesus' challenge to the Pharisees was so powerful. Jesus was calling on a group of people to humble themselves into the posture of students, even though they were supposed to be professor-level teachers of the law.

This episode in the Bible can be instructive for you and me. Each of us likely has parts of our faith that need to be revisited with deeper questions and more careful attention to God's heart and purpose. And maybe that was Jesus' ultimate goal: not for us all to have perfectly refined theology but for us to know the heart of our Savior. A knowing that is willing to let go of past perceptions and to welcome new understanding.

An important part of understanding the meaning of a Bible passage is getting a sense of its place in the broader storyline of Scripture. When we make connections between different parts of the Bible, we get a glimpse of the unity and cohesion of the Scriptures.

My son Caleb's appreciation for the author C. S. Lewis has deepened as he's been reading through The Chronicles of Narnia and discovering thematic patterns in the types of characters Lewis uses in his storytelling. Caleb was delighted and shocked when he realized that Aslan, the great Lion throughout the books, is like Jesus in the Bible.

Matthew the tax collector is a particular kind of character type in the Bible, joining a list of tax collectors who responded to Jesus with surrender, faith, and devotion. In Luke 18:9-14, Jesus tells his disciples a parable about a Pharisee and a tax collector. Notice with me all the literary parallels between this story and Matthew's.

7. **Read Luke 18:9-14. Underline any mention of a Pharisee, and circle any mention of a tax collector.**

9 He also told this parable to some who trusted in themselves that they were righteous and looked down on everyone else: 10 "Two men went up to the temple to pray, one a Pharisee and the other a tax collector. 11 The Pharisee was standing and praying like this about himself: 'God, I thank you that I'm not like other people—greedy, unrighteous, adulterers, or even like this tax collector. 12 I fast twice a week; I give a tenth of everything I get.'

13 "But the tax collector, standing far off, would not even raise his eyes to heaven but kept striking his chest and saying, 'God, have mercy on me, a sinner!' 14 I tell you, this one went down to his house justified rather than the other, because everyone who exalts himself will be humbled, but the one who humbles himself will be exalted."

LUKE 18:9-14

8. What was Jesus' point in this parable?

Luke 19:1-10 presents another Bible story about a tax collector repenting and believing in Christ. This tax collector's name was Zacchaeus, and like Matthew and the tax collector in Jesus' parable, Zacchaeus was willing to honor Christ in his profession and follow the way of Jesus.

9. Read Luke 19:1-10 and draw a bubble around Zacchaeus's words to Jesus.

19 He entered Jericho and was passing through. ² There was a man named Zacchaeus who was a chief tax collector, and he was rich. ³ He was trying to see who Jesus was, but he was not able because of the crowd, since he was a short man. ⁴ So running ahead, he climbed up a sycamore tree to see Jesus, since he was about to pass that way. ⁵ When Jesus came to the place, he looked up and said to him, "Zacchaeus, hurry and come down because today it is necessary for me to stay at your house."

⁶ So he quickly came down and welcomed him joyfully. ⁷ All who saw it began to complain, "He's gone to stay with a sinful man."

⁸ But Zacchaeus stood there and said to the Lord, "Look, I'll give half of my possessions to the poor, Lord. And if I have extorted anything from anyone, I'll pay back four times as much."

⁹ "Today salvation has come to this house," Jesus told him, "because he too is a son of Abraham. ¹⁰ For the Son of Man has come to seek and to save the lost."

LUKE 19:1-10

10. How did Zacchaeus show Jesus he was ready to follow the way of Christ?

We're going to look at one last group of tax collectors before we ponder how to apply these stories to our own lives: the tax collectors baptized by John the Baptist. In Luke 3, John the Baptist, a man who announced God's Kingdom through a message of repentance, was chastising people's unwillingness to repent. Some of the crowd gathered to hear John's message and started to ask John to tell them what repentance might look like in their specific situations. They asked, "What then should we do?" (Luke 3:10). By that they meant *What should we do to show we are truly repentant of our sins?* Among the diverse types of people in the crowd that day were some tax collectors.

The shocking outcome of the parable is that it is the tax collector, not the Pharisee, who goes away justified (i.e., vindicated as a covenant member in good standing) by the fact of his contrite disposition and self-humiliation. The striking message of the parable is that it is those who recognize God as a gracious benefactor and not themselves as worthy of divine benefaction who possess the appropriate mindset for those who seek to be at peace with God.[12]

Michael F. Bird, "Sin, Sinner," in *Dictionary of Jesus and the Gospels*

---

11. Read Luke 3:12-13 and underline what John told tax collectors to do to live repentantly.

¹² Tax collectors also came to be baptized, and they asked him, "Teacher, what should we do?"

   ¹³ He told them, "Don't collect any more than what you have been authorized."

LUKE 3:12-13

Some of us don't need to leave our professions—we need a change of heart. We need to wholeheartedly commit to living repentantly in the industries or life stages we find ourselves in. And the good news is that you and I have biblical examples of internalizing and embodying faith in Jesus while continuing on in our vocations. The tax collectors show us how.

◆ ◆ ◆

In each lesson, we will explore the Sinners Storyline to get a big-picture overview of what God is up to through the stories of the people we are studying together.

THE SINNERS STORYLINE OF SCRIPTURE

Character	Why were they considered sinful?	How did they act in faith?
the disciple named Matthew (Matthew 9)	Matthew was a tax collector, and tax collectors were some of the most hated people in Jesus' day because they worked for the Romans and often stole money.	Matthew left his tollbooth behind to follow Jesus.
a Roman centurion (Luke 7)	The Roman centurion represented both the Romans, who were in a political and religious tug-of-war with the Jews, and the military, which was enforcing oppression of the Jews.	The Roman centurion advocated for his sick servant.
a sinful woman (Luke 7)	We don't know anything about her life or why she was considered sinful, but the Bible says that this was her reputation.	The sinful woman anointed Jesus' feet with an alabaster jar of perfume in a generous act of devotion.
a Canaanite mom (Matthew 15)	The Canaanites were known as the people group occupying the Promised Land before the Israelites.	The Canaanite mom begged Jesus to heal her demon-possessed daughter.
the Samaritan woman at the well (John 4)	The Samaritans were hated by the Jews for religious and ethnic animosity. They were considered half-breeds and sinful for their rejection of the Jerusalem Temple.	The Samaritan woman at the well believed Jesus was the Savior of the world and proclaimed it to her city.

What did Jesus say to them?	Who are they compared to in their story?	What was the outcome of their faith?
"Follow me."	Matthew and his friends are contrasted with the unrepentant Pharisees.	Jesus welcomed Matthew into his inner circle of disciples, healing him from feeling hated.
"I have not found so great a faith even in Israel."	The Roman centurion is contrasted with the passive crowd following Jesus.	Jesus healed the Roman centurion's sick servant.
"Your faith has saved you. Go in peace."	The sinful woman's love is contrasted with Simon the Pharisee's stingy hosting.	Jesus forgave the woman's sins, healing her soul.
"Woman, your faith is great. Let it be done for you as you want."	The Canaanite mom is contrasted with the disciples.	Jesus healed the woman's daughter.
"I, the one speaking to you, am he."	The Samaritan woman at the well is contrasted with Nicodemus the Pharisee in John 3.	Jesus met the woman's needs and changed—or healed—her story.

1. What about Matthew's story resonates with you most?

2. What did you learn about God's character in this lesson?

3. How should these truths shape your faith community and change you?

RESPONDING

The purpose of Bible study is to help you become more Christlike; that's why part 4 will include journaling space for your reflection on and responses to the content and a blank checklist for actionable next steps. You'll be able to process what you're learning so that you can live out the concepts and pursue Christlikeness. Part 4 will enable you to answer the questions *What truths is this passage teaching?* and *How do I apply this to my life?*

MATTHEW IS ONLY MENTIONED a handful of times in the New Testament, but as one of Jesus' twelve disciples, he was likely present for many of the moments documented in the Gospel accounts. That means Matthew

- listened to Jesus teach parables,
- watched up close as Jesus healed the sick,
- witnessed the dead raised to new life,
- shared the gospel as an evangelist,
- agonized over Jesus' crucifixion,
- rejoiced over Jesus' resurrection, and
- received Jesus' commission to make disciples of all the nations.

Matthew's life was never the same after he chose to leave his tollbooth and follow Jesus. But there's also something that never changed about Matthew. He never dropped the title *tax collector*. In his own Gospel account, Matthew refers to himself as "Matthew the tax collector" even after coming to faith in Christ (Matthew 10:3).

His new identity was in Christ, but I'm curious whether Matthew considered his previous profession a part of himself. Not the whole. Not his identity. But a part of his past that he embraced without shame. He'd been forgiven and welcomed into Jesus' inner circle, befriended and loved unconditionally by his Savior. Matthew was secure in his new identity as a child of God, and his old profession was simply a part of his life. His past informed but did not define his future. It's the same for us. God—not what we do or what we've done—defines our identity.

Matthew found freedom in Christ, and we can discover a few insights from Matthew's willingness to abandon his post at the tollbooth and join Jesus' mission.

1. LEAVE YOUR TOLLBOOTH.

Tollbooths are whatever keeps us from following Jesus wholeheartedly. For some of us, our tollbooths are the taxing, sinful behaviors we still resist giving up. Whatever our vices, however they support our wayward living, they are boxing us in and keeping us from moving about freely in life. For others, our tollbooths represent oppressive business tactics that penalize the poor and perpetuate systemic disparities. Profiting off the poor in our industries is not the way of Christ. Jesus may be motioning you to abandon your post and to resist profits that neglect the marginalized. Do it. Leave your tollbooth. Participating in injustice seems like security, but really it's more like a holding cell, enslaving you to sin.

But some of us may have tollbooths that are not external. They are not looming structures calling attention to everyone who passes by. Instead, our taxes go to resentment, anger, and unforgiveness. Some of these internal struggles begin precisely because we are owed an emotional debt. But no amount of taxing ourselves or others is bringing us peace. To you I would say: Escape that wretched tollbooth. Stand up and take a step toward Jesus.

2. FOLLOW JESUS.

We do not follow denominations, churches' theological traditions, Christian celebrities, or even our faith leaders. You and I follow Jesus, the One and only. What is his opinion on the matter? How would he handle your situation? How did he model faithfulness in his life? What does he tell us to do and not to do? I want to encourage you to zero in on Christ and study him. Get in God's Word for the purpose of becoming more like Christ.

If the New Testament Gospel accounts show us anything, it's that following Jesus will be scary, unpredictable, risky, dangerous, and confusing. But it will always lead to love. Following Jesus will also be fulfilling, joyful, surprising, and encouraging. Best of all, following Jesus means you'll be close to him. This man who never jeers at women, oppresses the weak, or excludes the repentant sinner. This man who gives away his power, washes the feet of his loved ones, and gives his own life so that we can live. Follow *that guy*.

3. LIVE REPENTANTLY.

Matthew left his tollbooth at a moment in time, but he also chose to stay with Christ every day after. You and I have similar decisions to make. Not only do we have to leave our tollbooths and follow Jesus, but we also have to choose to live each day repentantly. To turn away from the confinements of sin and shame and turn toward Christ time and time again. To live repentantly is to change your mind about your tollbooth and change your ways into the ways of Christ. At times we will be tempted to turn back to see our tollbooths. Remember, the same motion that turns you to face your tollbooth can turn you right back around to see Jesus' face.

Use this journaling space to process what you are learning.

Ask yourself how these truths impact your relationship with God and with others.

What is the Holy Spirit bringing to your mind as actionable next steps in your faith journey?

- ◆
- ◆
- ◆

ADVOCATING FOR YOUR LOVED ONES WITH ALL YOU'VE GOT

THE ROMAN CENTURION:
THE FAITH OF THE OFFICER WHO ADVOCATES FOR HIS SICK SERVANT

SCRIPTURE: LUKE 7

PART 1

CONTEXT

Before you begin your study, we will start with the context of the story we are about to read together: the setting, both cultural and historical; the people involved; and where our passage fits in the larger setting of Scripture. All these things help us make sense of what we're reading. Understanding the context of a Bible story is fundamental to reading Scripture well. Getting your bearings before you read will enable you to answer the question *What am I about to read?*

THE BEST ADVOCATE I KNOW is one of my besties, Jenn Jett Barrett. She's on a mission to champion Christian leaders. Ask anyone in her orbit, and they'll tell you: Many of them launched into serving Christ because of her prayer and support. Jenn describes her passion as "dream defending" because she believes our dreams are God given.

Do you have someone in your life who has defended your dreams? Some of us had coaches who saw our potential in a sport or hobby. They took us under their wings and showed us what could be possible. Some of us had teachers or professors who pulled us aside and cast a vision for our future in academics. Others of us had parents or grandparents who championed our work long before we did anything noteworthy. Their advocacy got us where we are now.

When I posed the question *What makes a great advocate?* to some of my friends, here are some of the responses I received. Advocates . . .

- open doors,
- make introductions,
- cheer us up when we are discouraged,
- celebrate our successes,
- grieve our losses,
- see our work behind the scenes,
- affirm our value beyond what we do for God,
- refuse to let us quit, and
- help us get back up when we've been knocked down.

Isn't *that* the truth?

The best advocates believe us *and* believe in us. They specialize in spreading hope, and they're expert encouragers. Advocates rush to our sides and defend our dreams when our confidence is low. They remind us of God's Word, God's timing, and God's Son, Jesus. And they pray—with persistence, confidence, and faith. Advocates pray like all heaven is listening and nothing will get in God's way.

Jenn Jett Barrett came to mind every time I revisited the centurion's story in Luke 7 because both advocate for their loved ones with all they've got. Jenn advocates through a boutique gathering called The Well Summit, while the centurion advocated by leveraging his connections and recruiting his friends' help to ask for healing for his servant.

We're about to study the story of a Roman centurion, an officer in the Roman army, who had a sick servant. Most of the time when the New Testament mentions servants, the subject is slavery. This form of slavery was not exactly like the chattel slavery of the Western world, but that doesn't matter when both forms of oppression were based on one human being owning another. Unequivocally, slavery in every form is evil and antithetical to the God who releases captives and sets people free. Full stop.

Slavery is never endorsed in the Bible; it is a part of the cultural backdrop. We should read the Scriptures and bristle and anguish over the presence of slavery in the text. The Roman centurion who showed great faith in Christ and great compassion to his servant was a slave owner. Although the Scriptures do not tell us that this centurion abandoned the evil practice of slavery after coming to Christ in faith, I do have hope that we will get to heaven and learn of many slave owners who did just that.

Ironically, the centurion's peers considered him a sinner because he was a Roman, a representative of an empire that oppressed the Jews—*not* because he was a slave owner. There is a whole sermon in that tragic fact. But for now, I hope you don't look past the centurion's choice to enslave others. God included that point to confront us with reality and to teach us to live differently. Instead, I hope you will see the complexities of broken, sinful people coming to faith in Christ. The faithful, pious acts of this Roman centurion can teach us something about how to advocate for others with all we've got, *and* it can also serve as a reminder that no matter how much we do personally, we also need to be willing to abandon systems of oppression.

We're about to read a story about Christ's compassion for both the oppressed and the oppressor. It's a story full of tension: God can use us personally to help others, and at the same time we can be part of the system of violence that Christ will eventually dismantle. We are not going to study the centurion's great act of faith in isolation; we are going to connect his faithful actions to his belief in Christ. For anyone living a messy, complicated life: Read closely of God's tender-heartedness toward you.

1. **PERSONAL CONTEXT: What is going on in your life right now that might impact how you understand this Bible character?**

2. **SPIRITUAL CONTEXT: If you've never studied this Bible story before, what piques your curiosity? If you've studied this passage before, what impressions and insights do you recall?**

PART 2

SEEING

Seeing the text is vital if we want the heart of the Scripture passage to sink in. We read slowly and intentionally through the text with the context in mind. As we practice close, thoughtful reading of Scripture, we pick up on phrases, implications, and meanings we might otherwise have missed. Part 2 includes close Scripture reading and observation questions to empower you to answer the question *What is the story saying?*

1. **Read Luke 7:1-10 and underline everything the centurion does out of faith in Christ.**

7 When he had concluded saying all this to the people who were listening, he entered Capernaum. ² A centurion's servant, who was highly valued by him, was sick and about to die. ³ When the centurion heard about Jesus, he sent some Jewish elders to him, requesting him to come and save the life of his servant. ⁴ When they reached Jesus, they pleaded with him earnestly, saying, "He is worthy for you to grant this, ⁵ because he loves our nation and has built us a synagogue."

⁶ Jesus went with them, and when he was not far from the house, the centurion sent friends to tell him, "Lord, don't trouble yourself, since I am not worthy to have you come under my roof. ⁷ That is why I didn't even consider myself worthy to come to you. But say the word, and my servant

This confidence takes faith and humility, for the centurion is a man of standing in the community and his honor is at stake.[1]

Diane G. Chen, *Luke* (New Covenant Commentary Series)

will be healed. [8] For I too am a man placed under authority, having soldiers under my command. I say to this one, 'Go,' and he goes; and to another, 'Come,' and he comes; and to my servant, 'Do this,' and he does it."

[9] Jesus heard this and was amazed at him, and turning to the crowd following him, he said, "I tell you, I have not found so great a faith even in Israel." [10] When those who had been sent returned to the house, they found the servant in good health.

LUKE 7:1-10

The centurion heard, sent, requested, built, and sent again. He was a man full of action.

2. List both reasons the Jewish elders vouched for the Roman centurion.

1.

2.

This seems like an unlikely alliance—the Jews and a Roman centurion—but the Roman centurion loved the nation of Israel and had invested in their way of life by building a Jewish synagogue. He'd proven himself an ally of the Jewish people.

3. Why did the Roman centurion send the Jewish elders and not go to Christ himself?

4. **Describe a time when you felt unworthy to approach Christ. What was behind those feelings, and how did you respond?**

A centurion was a gentile who represented Rome's oppressive powers and would have been feared or hated by the Jews. The centurion in this story, however, breaks the stereotype.[2]

Diane G. Chen, *Luke* (New Covenant Commentary Series)

The Roman centurion chose not to approach Christ because he knew he was unworthy to. Luke, the author of this Gospel account, doesn't give us more insight into the centurion's insecurities. Were they humble affirmations of Christ's lordship and authority as the Messiah? Did they emerge from fear of Christ's judgment?

5. **Despite feeling unworthy, the Roman centurion was persistent in his advocacy for his sick servant. Not only did he send a group of Jewish elders to invite Jesus to heal his servant, but he also sent another group of people. Based on Luke 7:6, who else did the centurion send to Jesus?**

The centurion's actions remind me of times my son, Caleb, will ask his grandmother for something first and then ask his dad and then ask me. His three-pronged approach is persistent and sometimes effective. When my mom, my husband, and I compare notes on Caleb's requests, we usually smile with appreciation. We've got to hand it to Caleb—he's nothing if not determined. The Roman centurion exhibited determination too. He knew Jesus could save his servant. In fact, he knew Jesus didn't even have to be present to heal his servant. With just a word, the Lord Jesus could raise the dead to life and the sick to health.

6. Write out what the centurion says to Jesus in Luke 7:6.

"I am not worthy to have you _____."

The centurion, a man well acquainted with authority, recognized that Jesus is the ultimate authority. He deferred to him in humility, submission, and reverence. And he realized that even though he could relate to Jesus' power, there was no comparison.

7. Imagine what kind of testimony the centurion's friends and the servant's friends had after witnessing the miraculous healing of the servant. Write out a fictional account in the first person.

8. What impression did the centurion make on Jesus, based on Luke 7:9?

Jesus being amazed by one of his creatures mystifies me. Jesus was present at the inception of time, present when the foundations of the earth were formed. Jesus, wholly transcendent and infinitely powerful, speaks and worlds are ordered. And yet he has the capacity to be amazed. What does Jesus marvel at? What shocks his system and catches him off guard? The faith of a Roman centurion. Jesus' amazement is in sharp contrast to his indictment of Israel throughout the book of Luke. Simply put, the Israelites are out-faithed by a Roman soldier.

9. **What about the centurion's actions exemplified faith? List anything that comes to mind.**

10. **Look at your list above and circle any of the centurion's faithful actions that are similar to your own.**

It is no secret that I get hung up in Scripture often. I settle into a part of the Bible and feel as though I can't move on because I find the details so riveting. Luke 7 is one such spot for me. After hours of meditating on this story about the centurion's servant being healed, the one sentence I could not escape was "But say the word, and my servant will be healed" (Luke 7:7). These words from the centurion rang in my ear like an unending echo.

Our God can heal with words. By just one word, all creation yields to his will. And the centurion knew it. I'm not sure I do though. Conceptually, I have no doubt that God is all-powerful. Practically, I struggle with faith as strong as the centurion's.

Do we need to approach Jesus with more audacity? What would it look like to call upon Jesus to act on our behalf?

If the centurion was right—and we know he was—that Jesus can invoke healing privileges by saying a word, let's ask him right now for what we need. *Say the word, Lord, please.*

PART 3

UNDERSTANDING

Now that we've finished a close reading of the Scriptures, we're going to spend some time on interpretation: doing our best to understand what God was saying to the original audience and what he's teaching us through the process. But to do so, we need to learn his ways and consider how God's Word would have been understood by the original audience before applying the same truths to our own lives. "Scripture interpretation" may sound a little stuffy, but understanding what God means to communicate to us in the Bible is crucial to enjoying a close relationship with Jesus. Part 3 will enable you to answer the question *What does it mean?*

ONE DREAMY SUMMER, Aaron and I vacationed in a place that is like heaven on earth: the Guanacaste peninsula of Costa Rica. Watching the bright rays of the sun sinking into the ocean—behind a mountain, surrounded by plush vegetation—ranks as the single best sunset of our lives so far.

At one of our dinners, some strangers approached us. "We couldn't help but overhear your conversation," they said. They'd unintentionally listened to us discuss our plans for the next day. As locals, they had helpful tips for us to get the most out of our trip. I'm so glad they eavesdropped. Their recommendations took our excursions to the next level.

Many people were listening to Jesus' interactions with the centurion's friends. Luke makes a point to tell us that there was a crowd following Jesus during this episode, people who were absorbing the experience. These people couldn't help but overhear how Jesus responded to the request for healing. I wonder how Jesus' words impacted everyone within earshot: "I tell you, I have not found so great a faith even in Israel." I bet this declaration sent shock waves through the crowd—and marked their lives forever.

1. **How do you think this story impacted the Jewish elders and the centurion's friends who petitioned Jesus to heal the servant?**

The elders and other friends of the centurion were likely convinced that Jesus could help. I wonder if they started to make requests of Jesus themselves. In my own life, sometimes I need to see God work a miracle in someone else's situation before I trust him with my problems. It sounds silly, I know. But it's real. Every time I see God come through for others, my confidence in God is renewed. If we are struggling in our faith, we may need to be more intentional in asking our loved ones and friends to share their victories with us. And maybe we all need to start sharing our prayer requests before and after they get answered.

2. **What did Jesus mean when he said he had not yet found anyone in Israel with so great a faith?**
   □ Jesus was making a contrast between the faith of Israel and the faith of the centurion.
   □ Jesus was speaking in hyperbole to point out the great faith of the centurion.
   □ Both of the above.

> This expression of faith by a Gentile stands in sharp contrast to the rejection of Jesus by the Jewish religious leaders.[3]
>
> Takatemjen, "Luke," in *South Asia Bible Commentary*

MAKING CONNECTIONS

An important part of understanding the meaning of a Bible passage is getting a sense of its place in the broader storyline of Scripture. When we make connections between different parts of the Bible, we get a glimpse of the unity and cohesion of the Scriptures.

I watch a lot of Marvel movies in the theater on opening night, and one of the best parts is the final scene after the credits roll. You get a sneak peek into the character's next iteration. As the lights come up in the theater, Marvel fans buzz with enthusiasm about the glimpse of the unfolding story.

In the New Testament, the Roman centurion's story might unfold in a similar way. Although Luke seems to move on from this healing event in his Gospel account, centurions are mentioned a few more times in Scripture—and the thematic storyline has made me wonder more than once if they might all be the same person.

3. **Read Luke 23:44–49 and underline anything the centurion says during Jesus' crucifixion.**

⁴⁴ It was now about noon, and darkness came over the whole land until three, ⁴⁵ because the sun's light failed. The curtain of the sanctuary was split down the middle. ⁴⁶ And Jesus called out with a loud voice, "Father, into your hands I entrust my spirit." Saying this, he breathed his last.

⁴⁷ When the centurion saw what happened, he began to glorify God, saying, "This man really was righteous!" ⁴⁸ All the crowds that had gathered for this spectacle, when they saw what had taken place, went

home, striking their chests. [49] But all who knew him, including the women who had followed him from Galilee, stood at a distance, watching these things.

LUKE 23:44-49

4. What did the centurion do and say in this story?

We can't know for sure, but consider for a moment that this Roman centurion could be the same centurion from Luke 7. Wouldn't it make sense that the centurion's life would be so changed by his servant's healing that he would immediately glorify God and proclaim Jesus as righteous after Jesus' crucifixion?

Maybe since the centurion had seen his servant healed, he also anticipated a miraculous healing of the ultimate Servant, Jesus. Whether this is the same man or not, both centurions exhibited great faith in God.

As we shift gears and consider the impact the centurion's faith should have on our own lives, let's pay attention to the role this character plays in the New Testament. For all practical purposes, the Roman centurion was an enemy to God's people, an unlikely candidate for righteous living. But he shattered the stereotypes, proving that anyone who approaches God in faith will receive the life-saving gift of God's grace.

◆ ◆ ◆

Let's check back in on our Sinners Storyline.

THE SINNERS STORYLINE OF SCRIPTURE

Character	Why were they considered sinful?	How did they act in faith?
the disciple named Matthew (Matthew 9)	Matthew was a tax collector, and tax collectors were some of the most hated people in Jesus' day because they worked for the Romans and often stole money.	Matthew left his tollbooth behind to follow Jesus.
a Roman centurion (Luke 7)	The Roman centurion represented both the Romans, who were in a political and religious tug-of-war with the Jews, and the military, which was enforcing oppression of the Jews.	The Roman centurion advocated for his sick servant.
a sinful woman (Luke 7)	We don't know anything about her life or why she was considered sinful, but the Bible says that this was her reputation.	The sinful woman anointed Jesus' feet with an alabaster jar of perfume in a generous act of devotion.
a Canaanite mom (Matthew 15)	The Canaanites were known as the people group occupying the Promised Land before the Israelites.	The Canaanite mom begged Jesus to heal her demon-possessed daughter.
the Samaritan woman at the well (John 4)	The Samaritans were hated by the Jews for religious and ethnic animosity. They were considered half-breeds and sinful for their rejection of the Jerusalem Temple.	The Samaritan woman at the well believed Jesus was the Savior of the world and proclaimed it to her city.

What did Jesus say to them?	Who are they compared to in their story?	What was the outcome of their faith?
"Follow me."	Matthew and his friends are contrasted with the unrepentant Pharisees.	Jesus welcomed Matthew into his inner circle of disciples, healing him from feeling hated.
"I have not found so great a faith even in Israel."	The Roman centurion is contrasted with the passive crowd following Jesus.	Jesus healed the Roman centurion's sick servant.
"Your faith has saved you. Go in peace."	The sinful woman's love is contrasted with Simon the Pharisee's stingy hosting.	Jesus forgave the woman's sins, healing her soul.
"Woman, your faith is great. Let it be done for you as you want."	The Canaanite mom is contrasted with the disciples.	Jesus healed the woman's daughter.
"I, the one speaking to you, am he."	The Samaritan woman at the well is contrasted with Nicodemus the Pharisee in John 3.	Jesus met the woman's needs and changed—or healed—her story.

1. What about the Roman centurion's story resonates with you most?

2. What did you learn about God's character in this lesson?

3. How should these truths shape your faith community and change you?

RESPONDING

The purpose of Bible study is to help you become more Christlike; that's why part 4 will include journaling space for your reflection on and responses to the content and a blank checklist for actionable next steps. You'll be able to process what you're learning so that you can live out the concepts and pursue Christlikeness. Part 4 will enable you to answer the questions *What truths is this passage teaching?* and *How do I apply this to my life?*

ALMOST A DECADE AGO, my friend Jenn Jett Barrett sat with me in an empty ballroom for an hour after a keynote had ended. She had noticed someone in the room who needed some compassion and a listening ear: me. I was considering giving up on a dream. I dumped a lot on Jenn that day, but she took it all in stride and waited until I was out of words and out of tears. She leaned in, took my hand, and stared into my eyes, exhorting me not to give up on my dream. She was emphatic: "You can't give up."

This moment in our friendship was a fork in my road. The dream came to fruition because she just simply wouldn't give up on me or the vision in my heart.

Everybody needs a Jenn in their life: a fierce advocate gentle enough to speak into the tender parts of your story with grace and bold enough to defend your dreams.

Both Jenn and the Roman centurion knew how to be faithful in their advocacy. And both their lives can serve as a challenge to you and to me. Will we act faithfully? Will we choose to be an ally when someone needs to borrow from our faith?

Notice with me all the intentional ways the centurion acted on his faith in Christ:

- He had compassion on his servant's condition. Compassion fatigue is rampant in our lives because we've lived through such perilous times, but staying vigilant and continuing to offer our compassion to others is the way of Christ.

- He advocated for the servant's healing. The centurion did more than feel compassion; he acted on that conviction with advocacy.

- He leveraged all his connections and allies to benefit his sick servant.

- He created an interdependent network of relationships across cultural barriers. Although the Roman army and Jewish leaders were at odds culturally, the Roman centurion built bridges with perceived enemies to work toward the common good.

- He recognized that Jesus saves by the power of his word.

Before we consider different ways to internalize the Roman centurion's example, let's wrestle with some questions that will help us make our advocacy more tangible. I'll warn you: I tried to avoid the feelings of conviction these questions brought, but they wouldn't hush. I'm praying they help lead you to some next right steps to be a better advocate, just as they did for me.

1. **On a scale of 1 to 10, how would you rate yourself in the area of compassion (10 being very compassionate and 1 being not compassionate at all)?**

| 1 | 2 | 3 | 4 | 5 | 6 | 7 | 8 | 9 | 10 |

2. **How could you grow in compassion?**

3. **Who should you be advocating for right now? What would be the best way for you to do that?**

4. **Whom do you know who could help you advocate? List their names below.**

Now that you have some names and faces in mind, let's consider two foundational aspects of supporting those you love.

1. BELIEVE THAT JESUS SAVES.

You might be the best friend, spouse, roommate, teammate, or parent in the whole world—but you can't save someone. We've likely all attempted to rescue someone we love. It never works out, does it? Try as we might, we can't change someone's mind, protect them from life's challenges, or change the course of history. But Jesus can.

You and I are responsible for doing our part. If we can advocate, we should. But if someone needs a miracle, that's a job for Jesus. You and I need to believe that Jesus saves and to use that truth in our advocacy in the lives of our loved ones. If you wonder about the best way to advocate for someone, remind them that Jesus saves—and believe that truth with your whole heart.

2. TRUST THAT JESUS' WORDS ARE POWERFUL.

Caring advocates use their voices to speak life and advocate for justice. We've got to learn how to do so wisely, with truth and grace. But we shouldn't focus so heavily on our own voices that we minimize the power of Jesus' voice. Jesus says that he is the way, the truth, and the life (John 14:6). The Gospels show us time and time again that Jesus' words are powerful enough to calm the wind and the waves, to heal, and to save. When in doubt, advocate using the Word of God. Offer your support by passing along the words of Jesus. His words have unrivaled power.

Use this journaling space to process what you are learning.

Ask yourself how these truths impact your relationship with God and with others.

What is the Holy Spirit bringing to your mind as actionable next steps in your faith journey?

- ◆
- ◆
- ◆

OFFERING YOUR BEST TO GOD EVEN WHEN IT CAUSES A COMMOTION

THE SINFUL WOMAN:
THE FAITH OF THE OUTCAST WHO ANOINTS JESUS

SCRIPTURE: LUKE 7

PART 1

CONTEXT

Before you begin your study, we will start with the context of the story we are about to read together: the setting, both cultural and historical; the people involved; and where our passage fits in the larger setting of Scripture. All these things help us make sense of what we're reading. Understanding the context of a Bible story is fundamental to reading Scripture well. Getting your bearings before you read will enable you to answer the question *What am I about to read?*

MY FRIEND DAVID IS a man after God's own heart and a dedicated, godly worship leader. His artistic talents, generous spirit, and radical obedience make him an amazing leader from a platform. But I also know David as a caring friend. He's opened our family's eyes to beautiful expressions of faith in Christianity. My own tradition doesn't emphasize movement during worship songs in a church service. But in David's, jumping, shouting, and dancing are just things you do to praise God.

When David is in his element, worshiping God among Spirit-filled Christ followers, he moves carefree and uninhibited, singing and dancing. One Sunday, as my son, Caleb, observed David worshiping freely, he asked why David was moving to the beat of the drums. On the car ride home, we discussed different ways to show God our love.

We explained to Caleb that when David waves his arms or moves his feet in worship, that is the most genuine, natural expression of his faith. His love for Jesus compels him to lift his hands in adoration of his King. David isn't just feeling the music—he's expressing his experience of the saving power of Jesus in his personal life. David's whole body sings in concert with his affections for Christ. It's not the only way to worship, but it's David's.

If David exercised his freedom where I worship on Sunday mornings, he might, at first, be viewed by some with curiosity. Without some context, David's unfamiliar worship style might cause a commotion of sorts. Or it could be a catalyst for new and different ways to express devotion to Christ.

David's unhindered worship reminds me of the unnamed woman in Luke's Gospel who anointed Jesus' feet with perfume from an alabaster jar (Luke 7:36-50). In her case, her radical expression of faith disoriented the people around her. While her extravagant love for God spilled out of her alabaster jar and onto Jesus' feet, her actions caused controversy among those suspicious of Jesus.

To bring Simon to the place of self-examination, Jesus compares his behavior with that of the woman. One by one, Jesus names where Simon has fallen short as a host (7:44-46).[1]

Diane G. Chen, *Luke* (New Covenant Commentary Series)

We're about to turn to a Bible story also located in chapter 7 of the Gospel of Luke. The Gospel books of the Bible—Matthew, Mark, Luke, and John—are historical narratives or storied accounts of Jesus' life, death, and resurrection. The four Gospels include many of the same events, but they also reveal each author's unique perspective on Jesus' life and teachings.

The Luke identified as the author of this Gospel was likely a companion of the apostle Paul, who calls him a dear friend and a doctor in Colossians 4:14. Dr. Luke sequences his stories in a way that highlights several "righteous" sinners—people who had exemplary faith even though everybody else had already written them off.

You're about to study the story of a woman given one title in Scripture: *sinner*. We are not told why she carried such a shame-filled reputation, and we don't need to make assumptions to get the heart of the message.

Her story moves us beyond her past and the perceptions of her peers and into an embodied faith that broke through cultural and religious barriers.

You're going to notice her unstoppable audacity and her gumption to worship Jesus the best way she knew how. This story, and her character, could be an opportunity for you and me to emulate her faith and offer our best to God—even if it causes a disruption to our plans or reputations.

1. **PERSONAL CONTEXT: What is going on in your life right now that might impact how you understand this Bible character?**

2. **SPIRITUAL CONTEXT: If you've never studied this Bible story before, what piques your curiosity? If you've studied this passage before, what impressions and insights do you recall?**

PART 2

SEEING

Seeing the text is vital if we want the heart of the Scripture passage to sink in. We read slowly and intentionally through the text with the context in mind. As we practice close, thoughtful reading of Scripture, we pick up on phrases, implications, and meanings we might otherwise have missed. Part 2 includes close Scripture reading and observation questions to empower you to answer the question *What is the story saying?*

1. **Read Luke 7:36-50 and underline any part of the text that refers to the sinful woman.**

³⁶ Then one of the Pharisees invited [Jesus] to eat with him. He entered the Pharisee's house and reclined at the table. ³⁷ And a woman in the town who was a sinner found out that Jesus was reclining at the table in the Pharisee's house. She brought an alabaster jar of perfume ³⁸ and stood behind him at his feet, weeping, and began to wash his feet with her tears. She wiped his feet with her hair, kissing them and anointing them with the perfume.

³⁹ When the Pharisee who had invited him saw this, he said to himself, "This man, if he were a prophet, would know who and what kind of woman this is who is touching him—she's a sinner!"

⁴⁰ Jesus replied to him, "Simon, I have something to say to you."

He said, "Say it, teacher."

⁴¹ "A creditor had two debtors. One owed five hundred denarii, and the other fifty. ⁴² Since they could not pay it back, he graciously forgave them both. So, which of them will love him more?"

⁴³ Simon answered, "I suppose the one he forgave more."

"You have judged correctly," he told him. ⁴⁴ Turning to the woman, he said to Simon, "Do you see this woman? I entered your house; you gave me no water for my feet, but she, with her tears, has washed my feet and wiped them with her hair. ⁴⁵ You gave me no kiss, but she hasn't stopped kissing my feet since I came in. ⁴⁶ You didn't anoint my head with olive oil, but she has anointed my feet with perfume. ⁴⁷ Therefore I tell you, her many sins have been forgiven; that's why she loved much. But the one who is forgiven little, loves little." ⁴⁸ Then he said to her, "Your sins are forgiven."

⁴⁹ Those who were at the table with him began to say among themselves, "Who is this man who even forgives sins?"

⁵⁰ And he said to the woman, "Your faith has saved you. Go in peace."

LUKE 7:36-50

2. **Look up Luke 7:31-34. These words from Jesus directly lead into Luke's story of the sinful woman anointing Jesus' feet. What was Jesus' point in these verses? List the things you learn, or rephrase the point in your own words.**

After Jesus spoke to the crowds about their refusal to accept John the Baptist as a prophet, he chided them for being unwilling to repent of unrighteousness. Then he launched into a parable about the crowds missing the point. These people were an unresponsive generation. The sinful woman stands in stark contrast to them: She responded extravagantly.

3. List at least five things you learn about the sinful woman from this story:

1.

2.

3.

4.

5.

In the seventh chapter of his Gospel, Luke joins several important stories together, one of which is about a widow in a town called Nain whose son was in his coffin. Jesus intercepted the funeral procession and told the dead son to get up—and he did!

I'm curious about whether the sinful woman had any connection to the widow in Nain, since Luke places her story is such close proximity to the story of the sinful woman. Perhaps the miraculous resurrection of the widow's son so impacted the sinful woman that she was compelled to anoint Jesus in response.

And how did she find out that Jesus was dining with Simon? Was she asking around? Following him already? Did someone come and find her and tell her where Jesus would be? I have so many questions for her when we get to glory.

Whatever her previous experience with Jesus, the sinful woman came to him knowing there was only one way she could respond to his presence: to offer worship. She entered the house ready to shower Jesus with her appreciation and reverence.

The woman is carrying the ancient equivalent of Chanel No. 5.[2]

Amy-Jill Levine and Ben Witherington III,
The Gospel of Luke

4. How do you prefer to worship God? Through your work? Parenting? Singing? List any of the ways you worship God.

5. List at least five things you learn about Simon from this story:

    1.

    2.

    3.

    4.

    5.

6. Read Luke 7:39. Why do you think the Pharisee, Simon, hosted this dinner party?

Simon needed to see for himself what Jesus was really like. He'd likely heard Jesus teach and seen him heal the sick, but those things hadn't been enough to satisfy Simon's questions about whether Jesus was truly a prophet. That's the irony: The religious man got a close-up of Jesus but didn't really see things clearly; the sinful woman stepped forward with her exemplary faith despite only having seen Jesus from afar.

7. **Use the chart below to contrast Simon's reception of Jesus in his home with the sinful woman's offering of worship.**

Simon the Pharisee	The Sinful Woman
"You gave me no water for my feet." (Luke 7:44)	
"You gave me no kiss." (Luke 7:45)	
"You didn't anoint my head with olive oil." (Luke 7:46)	

The sinful woman's goal was to worship her Savior. Simon's goal was to figure out if Jesus was really a prophet. Her faith was evident to all, and the people surrounding her could have been marveling at her grand gesture. Instead, they were questioning Jesus' prophetic credentials. And if I'm honest, I relate more closely to the reserved, skeptical mindset of Simon and his dinner guests than that of the uninvited, sinful woman eager to declare her devotion to Christ. Sometimes we get so caught up in the to-dos and don'ts of our religion, we can miss the Jesus we follow.

Dr. Luke gives us several sensory details about this dinner party. We can imagine the fragrance of the food and drinks being served, but Luke also points us to the scent of perfume being poured out over Jesus' feet. The room would have been filled with the sound of conversation, but Luke highlights the sounds of the woman weeping and kissing Jesus' feet. I wonder how loudly she cried and kissed.

The sights, smells, and sounds of the evening likely stayed with the dinner guests long after they left.

8. If you were a character in this story, who would you be? Why?

☐ The sinful woman because _____

☐ Simon because _____

☐ The dinner guests because _____

9. How would you describe the way you worship God? Why?

☐ Extravagant because _____

☐ Generous because _____

☐ Suspicious because _____

☐ Something else because _____

Simon's dinner party was quite different from the dinners you and I host. Dr. Luke doesn't call it a potluck, and no one was making reservations on OpenTable or using a cash app to split the cost of eating out. And "reclining at the table"? Those of us from the West can't imagine eating while reclining unless we're in a La-Z-Boy chair.

Some of the elements of this story are challenging to decipher since so much time and space separate us from these ancient events. But one thing that has not changed over the centuries is the assumption that guests should be treated hospitably. We may not wash the feet of our dinner guests anytime soon, but the universal principle of being a generous host will never change. And Simon missed the mark. He hosted the King of the universe, the Savior of the world, and failed to honor him with generosity.

Whether Simon was obstinate and resisting hospitable behavior or simply distracted by his suspicions of Jesus, we don't know. But what I know for sure is that I don't want to treat Jesus the way Simon treated Jesus. I'm not sure I have the capacity or courage to approach Jesus with the sinful woman's unhindered worship, but I want to try.

PART 3

UNDERSTANDING

Now that we've finished a close reading of the Scriptures, we're going to spend some time on interpretation: doing our best to understand what God was saying to the original audience and what he's teaching us through the process. But to do so, we need to learn his ways and consider how God's Word would have been understood by the original audience before applying the same truths to our own lives. "Scripture interpretation" may sound a little stuffy, but understanding what God means to communicate to us in the Bible is crucial to enjoying a close relationship with Jesus. Part 3 will enable you to answer the question *What does it mean?*

MY HUSBAND, AARON, has gone on some short-term mission trips to both India and Africa. When he returns, all he can talk about is the generous hospitality of in-country leaders. The irony, Aaron points out, is that the trips are intended to provide encouragement and support to the national ministry leaders, but he always feels as though he offers less to the leaders than they offer to him through hospitality.

Christians have opened their homes to him, a stranger, and practically offered the clothes off their backs to make sure he has everything he needs during his stays. Even if his hosts were living in abject poverty, they always seemed to have enough to share when Aaron was hungry.

Aaron says the leaders he's been privileged to meet on his trips have unrivaled joy, and it shows up in jubilant praises to God at their church gatherings. Without exception, the leaders attribute their contentment and appreciation for life to their Savior, Jesus.

These radical displays of generosity have changed Aaron, and his stories challenge me to live on less and appreciate more. But also—I find myself reconsidering how generosity is tied to grace. I think this is the point Jesus makes in the parable he shares with Simon. Jesus uses the sinful woman's faith as an object lesson on generosity. Here's the zinger: Our generosity is proportional to our recognition of God's grace.

1. **Reread Luke 7:40-50. This time, circle the parts of the parable that represent the sinful woman and underline the parts of the parable that represent Simon.**

40 Jesus replied to him, "Simon, I have something to say to you."

He said, "Say it, teacher."

41 "A creditor had two debtors. One owed five hundred denarii, and the other fifty. 42 Since they could not pay it back, he graciously forgave them both. So, which of them will love him more?"

43 Simon answered, "I suppose the one he forgave more."

"You have judged correctly," he told him. 44 Turning to the woman, he said to Simon, "Do you see this woman? I entered your house; you gave me no water for my feet, but she, with her tears, has washed my feet and wiped them with her hair. 45 You gave me no kiss, but she hasn't stopped kissing my feet since I came in. 46 You didn't anoint my head with olive oil, but she has anointed my feet with perfume. 47 Therefore I tell you, her many sins have been forgiven; that's why she loved much. But the one who is forgiven little, loves little." 48 Then he said to her, "Your sins are forgiven."

49 Those who were at the table with him began to say among themselves, "Who is this man who even forgives sins?"

50 And he said to the woman, "Your faith has saved you. Go in peace."

LUKE 7:40-50

> The woman had the trust that, even if other people refused to forgive her and insist[ed] on seeing her as a sinner, Jesus would grant what they could not.[3]
>
> Amy-Jill Levine and Ben Witherington III, *The Gospel of Luke*

2. **Why do you think Jesus used this parable in this situation?**

3. **How do you think Simon and the dinner guests responded to the parable?**

4. **Jesus told the sinful woman to "go in peace" (Luke 7:50). In your experience, what does peace sound like and feel like? How might the sinful woman have experienced peace after this encounter with Jesus?**

> Jesus is making a connection between the cancellation of debt and the forgiveness of sins, with God as the benevolent creditor and the woman as the debtor with a large debt.[4]
>
> Diane G. Chen, *Luke* (New Covenant Commentary Series)

Sometimes, faith looks like anointing our King's feet. The sinful woman's faith compelled her to get low enough to express her deepest gratitude, and her King met her with compassion and peace. Are we willing to get low enough to receive peace?

MAKING CONNECTIONS

An important part of understanding the meaning of a Bible passage is getting a sense of its place in the broader storyline of Scripture. When we make connections between different parts of the Bible, we get a glimpse of the unity and cohesion of the Scriptures.

The sinful woman's willingness to lower herself in Christ's presence should prick our consciences—her humility is beautiful and inspiring. In even greater measure, our Savior, Jesus, was also willing to posture himself in humility when he washed his disciples' feet. Jesus didn't pour out oil from an alabaster jar like the sinful woman did, but he did kneel low and wipe the dirt off the soles of his disciples' feet in John 13.

Jesus' deference and humility during the foot washing is so jarring to Peter, so disruptive to his understanding of power and kingship, that he doesn't accept his kindness readily. In fact, he rejects Jesus' offer to wash his feet. Jesus does it anyway. He lays aside the clothing that restricts his movement so that he can get close enough to the disciples' feet to cover them in water and wipe away the grime with his own towel.

5. Read John 13:12-15 and circle the titles Jesus gives himself as he teaches his disciples the meaning of his foot-washing ceremony.

¹² When Jesus had washed their feet and put on his outer clothing, he reclined again and said to them, "Do you know what I have done for you? ¹³ You call me Teacher and Lord—and you are speaking rightly, since that is what I am. ¹⁴ So if I, your Lord and Teacher, have washed your feet, you also ought to wash one another's feet. ¹⁵ For I have given you an example, that you also should do just as I have done for you."

JOHN 13:12-15

6. Why do you think Jesus gives the disciples this example? Why do you think he teaches this lesson in this way?

Some of Jesus' disciples would have been present when the sinful woman anointed Jesus' feet with perfume from her alabaster jar. I imagine that during the foot-washing ceremony, they were envisioning all the times they'd seen someone else get low to the ground. Now, with stunning humility, Jesus was doing the same.

And so should we.

◆ ◆ ◆

Let's check back in on our Sinners Storyline.

THE SINNERS STORYLINE OF SCRIPTURE

Character	Why were they considered sinful?	How did they act in faith?
the disciple named Matthew (Matthew 9)	Matthew was a tax collector, and tax collectors were some of the most hated people in Jesus' day because they worked for the Romans and often stole money.	Matthew left his tollbooth behind to follow Jesus.
a Roman centurion (Luke 7)	The Roman centurion represented both the Romans, who were in a political and religious tug-of-war with the Jews, and the military, which was enforcing oppression of the Jews.	The Roman centurion advocated for his sick servant.
a sinful woman (Luke 7)	We don't know anything about her life or why she was considered sinful, but the Bible says that this was her reputation.	The sinful woman anointed Jesus' feet with an alabaster jar of perfume in a generous act of devotion.
a Canaanite mom (Matthew 15)	The Canaanites were known as the people group occupying the Promised Land before the Israelites.	The Canaanite mom begged Jesus to heal her demon-possessed daughter.
the Samaritan woman at the well (John 4)	The Samaritans were hated by the Jews for religious and ethnic animosity. They were considered half-breeds and sinful for their rejection of the Jerusalem Temple.	The Samaritan woman at the well believed Jesus was the Savior of the world and proclaimed it to her city.

What did Jesus say to them?	Who are they compared to in their story?	What was the outcome of their faith?
"Follow me."	Matthew and his friends are contrasted with the unrepentant Pharisees.	Jesus welcomed Matthew into his inner circle of disciples, healing him from feeling hated.
"I have not found so great a faith even in Israel."	The Roman centurion is contrasted with the passive crowd following Jesus.	Jesus healed the Roman centurion's sick servant.
"Your faith has saved you. Go in peace."	The sinful woman's love is contrasted with Simon the Pharisee's stingy hosting.	Jesus forgave the woman's sins, healing her soul.
"Woman, your faith is great. Let it be done for you as you want."	The Canaanite mom is contrasted with the disciples.	Jesus healed the woman's daughter.
"I, the one speaking to you, am he."	The Samaritan woman at the well is contrasted with Nicodemus the Pharisee in John 3.	Jesus met the woman's needs and changed—or healed—her story.

1. What about the sinful woman's story resonates with you most?

2. What did you learn about God's character in this lesson?

3. How should these truths shape your faith community and change you?

RESPONDING

The purpose of Bible study is to help you become more Christlike; that's why part 4 will include journaling space for your reflection on and responses to the content and a blank checklist for actionable next steps. You'll be able to process what you're learning so that you can live out the concepts and pursue Christlikeness. Part 4 will enable you to answer the questions *What truths is this passage teaching?* and *How do I apply this to my life?*

WE RECENTLY TOOK CALEB to see Dude Perfect, a group of YouTubers famous for their trick shots, live. Here's Caleb's review of the show: "EPIC!!!!!!!!" It was just us and about twenty thousand other people enjoying the camp-level energy coming from the stage. I agree with Caleb, the show was great, but getting out of the parking lot took f-o-r-e-v-e-r. Eventually, we decided to repark the car and wait out the crowds so that we could move forward in lighter traffic.

The sinful woman's story was so compelling, so life altering for me, that it halted my writing schedule and delayed this project by a few weeks. I had to park and wait in Luke 7 until I was supposed to move on. The Spirit needed more time with me—and, I believe, needed me to spend more time learning from the sinful woman's story.

Here are some truths from the sinful woman's story that resonated with me most. I hope they encourage you as well.

> The whole episode functions as an open-ended parable that confronts the hearer both then and now with making a decision to see as Jesus sees.[5]

Barbara E. Reid and Shelly Matthews, *Luke 1–9* (Wisdom Commentary)

1. JESUS OFFERS YOU THE DIGNITY OF BEING SEEN EVEN THOUGH YOU'VE BEEN MISUNDERSTOOD OR IGNORED.

We never forget the people who dignify our existence. The folks who look us in the eye, welcome our presence, and remind us that we belong. These people remind us of our image-bearing status, our sacred role in God's Kingdom, and our irreplaceable presence in the world. Those folks have a way of holding a mirror in front of our faces and pointing to our reflection with the truth: *Made in God's image. Worthy of God's love. Hardwired for connection with God.* And we love them for it, don't we?

In a world so determined to undervalue our significance, so intent on burdening us with shame, Jesus comes along and welcomes us all into his presence. Jesus offers us dignity, like he did for the sinful woman. He offers us the gift of being noticed, like he did for the sinful woman. And he offers us the joy of being understood.

If you've been misunderstood or ignored, I'm sorry. I know how easily those dehumanizing experiences can harden a heart. But stay tender. Stay gentle. Because the dignity Jesus offers is yours for the taking.

2. JESUS OFFERS YOU FORGIVENESS OF SINS EVEN THOUGH IT COST HIM HIS LIFE.

The sinful woman knew how much she needed to be saved from, and she knew that Jesus was the only One who could save. She was so sure of Jesus' ability to rescue her from sin, she disrupted a dinner party to express her gratitude. Jesus had not yet gone to the cross to pay for the sins of the world, yet the sinful woman had enough to go on. She knew that Jesus would offer her the peace that comes when you've been forgiven.

You and I know far more than the sinful woman did. We can read her story knowing that Jesus did eventually go to the cross, die a sinner's death, and then conquer sin and death through his resurrection. We know Jesus gave up his life to save ours. Yes, the sinful woman's offering was astounding and radically extravagant, but Jesus offering his own life was an even greater display of love and sacrifice.

Don't forget: Jesus offers you the forgiveness of your sins even though it cost him his life. And he would have it no other way. He would have done it just for you. Why not accept his forgiveness and go forward in peace?

3. FAITH INVOLVES OFFERING YOUR BEST TO GOD EVEN THOUGH IT CAUSES A COMMOTION.

Serving Jesus is going to cause a commotion. If you choose to bring your very best to God—I'm talking about radical obedience to his truth, unswerving devotion to the Holy Spirit's nudging, total commitment to love God and love others—things are going to get messy. As messy as an unwanted, uninvited guest who interrupts a dinner party to anoint Jesus' feet. Bring your best to God anyway. You might get the side-eye from well-intentioned Christians confused by your single-minded focus on God's mission. You might hear rumors that you've taken the gospel too far. You might second-guess your timing and question whether your offering even matters. Bring your best to Jesus anyway. Because you know that if you do, you'll enjoy the peace of God. Your humility and sacrifices might cause a commotion around you, but inside you'll have the peace that transcends understanding. The peace of knowing you gave Jesus the overflow of your heart. Wherever you go, however you serve Christ, you'll hear the words *Go in peace*.

The woman's limitless affection for Jesus is a model of what our response to God should be.[6]

Takatemjen, "Luke," in *South Asia Bible Commentary*

Use this journaling space to process what you are learning.

Ask yourself how these truths impact your relationship with God and with others.

What is the Holy Spirit bringing to your mind as actionable next steps in your faith journey?

-
-
-

PETITIONING JESUS FOR YOUR DEEPEST NEEDS

**THE CANAANITE MOM:
THE FAITH OF THE MOTHER WHO BEGS
JESUS TO HEAL HER POSSESSED DAUGHTER**

SCRIPTURE: MATTHEW 15

PART 1

CONTEXT

Before you begin your study, we will start with the context of the story we are about to read together: the setting, both cultural and historical; the people involved; and where our passage fits in the larger setting of Scripture. All these things help us make sense of what we're reading. Understanding the context of a Bible story is fundamental to reading Scripture well. Getting your bearings before you read will enable you to answer the question *What am I about to read?*

WE USED TO ATTEND A CHURCH that was so devoted to depending on Jesus, they added this phrase to their mission statement: *desperate dependence.* In an age and in a city puffed up with self-reliance and self-sufficiency, it felt inspiring to be a part of a local church that wanted to go against the status quo—to own its neediness.

But I was still caught off guard the first time I read that we as a church were going to celebrate our desperate dependence on Jesus and invite others to do the same. It made sense to me as a theme for the church as a whole, but for myself? I'm embarrassed to admit it—reliance on Christ felt uncomfortable and counterintuitive.

I eventually decided that I was fine with the fact that I *needed* God. But my faith wasn't strong enough or humble enough to celebrate that I needed him *desperately.* In some upside-down way, I used to believe that becoming more godly would make Christians less needy.

The truth is, the more committed we become to Jesus and his ways, the more likely we are to realize just how much we must *desperately* depend on his Spirit to help us.

Real talk: I'm still allowing the Spirit to undo some self-reliance in my life. This will be a lifelong pursuit for me, I am sure. And what I found adjacent to self-reliance was judgmentalism. Not only did I not want to admit my ongoing desperation for Jesus, but I judged neediness in others, too.

I didn't just judge my ability (or lack thereof) to handle my own needs; when a need would arise in someone else's life, I used to think, *They need to get themselves together.*

I know I am not alone in this struggle. You might share it with me. And I think Jesus' disciples wrestled with self-sufficiency, too, based on the story Matthew shares in his Gospel about a Canaanite mom who throws herself at Jesus' feet to plead for her demon-possessed daughter's healing. The Canaanite mom's undignified and disruptive way of getting Jesus' attention would have made me uncomfortable at the very least. Maybe I would have pitied her cries for help, but I wonder if I would have thought, *Get it together, lady.*

Historically, the Canaanites were the group of people who lived in the land God had promised to the Israelites in the Old Testament. The Canaanites worshiped false gods, and their occupation of the Promised Land made them the Israelites' enemy. The Canaanites stood in the way of God's people claiming their God-given destiny. I find it fascinating that the Canaanite mom stands in the way of Jesus and his disciples too.

What you are about to read is a story about a mom who would do anything to save her daughter. Maybe you know what it feels like to be so devoted to someone you love that you would do literally anything to help them. You know the agony of trying multiple solutions, expensive ones, and still coming up without answers. You know the terror of worrying nonstop about the well-being of

> The woman's clever response displays her great and tenacious faith (v. 28), which contrasts with that of the disciples, whose fearfulness so often displays their "little faith" (6:30; 8:26; 14:31; 16:8; 17:20).[1]
>
> Barbara E. Reid, *The Gospel according to Matthew*

your loved one and the twenty-four seven vigilance required to make sure they are safe. Desperate times, desperate measures, right?

However and wherever we feel helpless in life, the Canaanite mom's example shows us that we don't need to get ourselves together. We need to get ourselves in front of Jesus and petition him about our greatest needs. I hope Jesus' response will tenderly encourage you to keep insisting God do something to help you. Don't give up.

1. **PERSONAL CONTEXT: What is going on in your life right now that might impact how you understand this Bible character?**

2. **SPIRITUAL CONTEXT: If you've never studied this Bible story before, what piques your curiosity? If you've studied this passage before, what impressions and insights do you recall?**

SEEING

Seeing the text is vital if we want the heart of the Scripture passage to sink in. We read slowly and intentionally through the text with the context in mind. As we practice close, thoughtful reading of Scripture, we pick up on phrases, implications, and meanings we might otherwise have missed. Part 2 includes close Scripture reading and observation questions to empower you to answer the question *What is the story saying?*

1. **Read Matthew 15:21-28 and color-code the conversation. Use one color to highlight or underline everything the Canaanite mom said. Use another color to highlight or underline everything Jesus said. Finally, use a third color to highlight or underline what the disciples said during this episode.**

²¹ When Jesus left there, he withdrew to the area of Tyre and Sidon.
²² Just then a Canaanite woman from that region came and kept crying out, "Have mercy on me, Lord, Son of David! My daughter is severely tormented by a demon."

²³ Jesus did not say a word to her. His disciples approached him and urged him, "Send her away because she's crying out after us."

²⁴ He replied, "I was sent only to the lost sheep of the house of Israel."

²⁵ But she came, knelt before him, and said, "Lord, help me!"

[26] He answered, "It isn't right to take the children's bread and throw it to the dogs."

[27] "Yes, Lord," she said, "yet even the dogs eat the crumbs that fall from their masters' table."

[28] Then Jesus replied to her, "Woman, your faith is great. Let it be done for you as you want." And from that moment her daughter was healed.

MATTHEW 15:21-28

In the first fifteen chapters of Matthew's Gospel, Jesus had been teaching and healing, but with a focus only on the Jews. God's plan had always included reaching Gentiles with the gospel message, but it seems clear that Jesus had a timetable that involved reaching the Jews first. That's part of what makes the Canaanite mom's request so audacious. She was a Gentile; it wasn't her turn yet. Her faith interrupted Jesus' Jewish-focused ministry with a cry for help.

Chapters before Jesus' conversation with the Canaanite mom, he'd finished preaching his most famous sermon, called the Sermon on the Mount. I marvel at the artistic brilliance present in God's storytelling through Matthew. First Jesus preached a sermon on a mount, and then he served a meal on a mount, feeding over five thousand people with just a few pieces of bread. In between those two events is the story of the Canaanite mom—and a conversation she had with Christ about breadcrumbs.

2. **List anything you know about the Canaanite mom below:**

    ◆

    ◆

    ◆

    ◆

3. **List all the things you wish you knew about this woman's story and the story of her daughter:**

    ◆

    ◆

◆

◆

◆

I wonder about this Canaanite mom's marriage, financial solvency, mental well-being, and childcare arrangements. Had mothering a demon-possessed child ruined her relationships? Had she spent everything she had on finding healing for her daughter? Was she depressed, lonely, exhausted? And who was watching her daughter when she petitioned Jesus? Whom could she trust with a demon-possessed child?

4. Write out the first sentence of Matthew 15:23 below.

❝

❞

5. What emotions do you feel knowing that Jesus didn't initially respond to the woman's request?

☐ I don't feel one way or another about Jesus' response.

☐ I'm confused.

☐ I'm frustrated.

☐ I'm angry.

☐ I'm surprised.

☐ Other:

Jesus tested some of his disciples with questions and others with silence. I wonder if he was creating space for this mom's faith to be shown.

6. **What do you imagine the woman was doing as she cried out to Jesus?**

    ☐ sobbing

    ☐ shouting

    ☐ begging

    ☐ reaching out her hands

    ☐ other:

Her interruption, her petition, was full of strength and intensity. *No, not later—right now. My daughter needs healing* now.

7. **According to Matthew 15:25, how did she posture herself as she begged?**

I have to wonder, how much fabric did she move to get low? How much dust unsettled when her knees hit the earth? How many people watched her undignified petition? This kneeling posture was the desperate plea of a woman unshaken by Jesus' faith test. She would not be moved until her daughter was healed.

If you need God's help today, let your body reflect the posture of your heart—unmoved by fear, doubt, or silence.

The Canaanite woman, like the centurion, is an outsider who humbles herself. This is why she is the only other figure in the Gospel whose faith is described as great.[2]

Michael Joseph Brown, "Matthew," in *True to Our Native Land*

PART 3

UNDERSTANDING

Now that we've finished a close reading of the Scriptures, we're going to spend some time on interpretation: doing our best to understand what God was saying to the original audience and what he's teaching us through the process. But to do so, we need to learn his ways and consider how God's Word would have been understood by the original audience before applying the same truths to our own lives. "Scripture interpretation" may sound a little stuffy, but understanding what God means to communicate to us in the Bible is crucial to enjoying a close relationship with Jesus. Part 3 will enable you to answer the question *What does it mean?*

SEVERAL PARTS OF the Canaanite mom's story seem cringeworthy, but the one I get hung up on is Jesus' suggestion that she was like a dog. What did Jesus mean by this?

Jesus and I are going to need a conversation in glory about his use of this imagery in his interaction with the Canaanite mom. And yet the strangeness of it should give us a clue that something else is going on. Whenever we are confused about what Jesus is saying in the Bible, we can look to other Scriptures to find truth that will help us interpret the meaning.

You and I know for sure that Jesus is God and that God is love (1 John 4:8). Anything he did or didn't do in his time on earth was consistent with his love, even if his actions don't make sense to us. We can be certain, based on what the whole of Scripture tells us about the character of God and his heart for the vulnerable

> Yet even this unflattering comparison is not enough to deter the woman. She stays with the analogy to advocate for her daughter (Matt 15:27).[3]

Jeannine K. Brown and Kyle Roberts, *Matthew*

and downtrodden (James 1:27), that Jesus had compassion on the woman in this passage, which means that he was not dismissing her the way the disciples did.

We also know that Jesus was having this conversation in front of his uncompassionate disciples. Could it be that Jesus was testing her faith and at the same time teaching his disciples a lesson about the Gentiles? Jesus tested her faith by bringing up a metaphor the Jews accepted about the Gentiles: that they were like dogs, unworthy of scraps from the table.

1. **How did the Canaanite mom respond to Jesus' analogy about dogs? Write out what she says in Matthew 15:27 below.**

"

"

2. **What do you think the disciples were thinking as the woman answered Jesus? Check all that apply.**
   - ☐ *How dare she?*
   - ☐ *What gall! What nerve! What audacity!*
   - ☐ *She's breaking rank.*
   - ☐ *She's talking back.*
   - ☐ *She's answering wisely.*

Her response was daring, audacious, a tad insubordinate—and yet wise. She knew that even the dogs get to eat the crumbs from the table. Despite the way the people of God perceived her people, she persistently, aggressively petitioned Jesus for mercy.

This Canaanite mom may not have known anything about the Old Testament of the Bible or the faith history of the Jewish people. But if she did, she would have known . . .

- Even a "dead dog" once ate at the king's table (2 Samuel 9:8).
- In Christ's name Gentiles will have hope (see Isaiah 42).

And if she had been following Jesus long enough to hear his Sermon on the Mount, she would know that those who hunger and thirst for righteousness will be filled. She would have heard Christ's instructions to pray for daily bread. Her persistence would have emerged not simply from the moment but from the larger picture of what she knew about Jesus—just as ours must.

3. **Why did Jesus tell the Canaanite mom that her faith was "great" in Matthew 15:28? What about her faith was great?**

4. **Describe what you imagine the woman's response was when Jesus healed her daughter.**

Did she burst into uncontrollable happy tears? Did she run home swiftly? Her faith had been proven strong before Jesus' disciples, and her daughter was healed. Jesus had given her what she'd asked for.

MAKING CONNECTIONS

An important part of understanding the meaning of a Bible passage is getting a sense of its place in the broader storyline of Scripture. When we make connections between different parts of the Bible, we get a glimpse of the unity and cohesion of the Scriptures.

---

5. **Read Matthew 15:29-37, which comes right after the Canaanite mom's story, and underline any mention of bread.**

29 Moving on from there, Jesus passed along the Sea of Galilee. He went up on a mountain and sat there, 30 and large crowds came to him, including the lame, the blind, the crippled, those unable to speak, and many others. They put them at his feet, and he healed them. 31 So the crowd was amazed when they saw those unable to speak talking, the crippled restored, the lame walking, and the blind seeing, and they gave glory to the God of Israel.

32 Jesus called his disciples and said, "I have compassion on the crowd, because they've already stayed with me three days and have nothing to eat. I don't want to send them away hungry, otherwise they might collapse on the way."

33 The disciples said to him, "Where could we get enough bread in this desolate place to feed such a crowd?"

34 "How many loaves do you have?" Jesus asked them.

"Seven," they said, "and a few small fish."

35 After commanding the crowd to sit down on the ground, 36 he took the seven loaves and the fish, gave thanks, broke them, and gave them to the disciples, and the disciples gave them to the crowds. 37 They all ate and were satisfied. They collected the leftover pieces—seven large baskets full.

MATTHEW 15:29-37

Jesus didn't want to send the crowd away hungry. The same compassion he felt for the Canaanite mom and for the disciples he had for those waiting to be healed on the mountainside.

6. Why didn't Jesus want to send the crowds away hungry (Matthew 15:32)?

7. What concerned the disciples in Matthew 15:33?

The disciples missed the significance of the Canaanite woman's faith. They asked Jesus *where* they could get enough bread in such a desolate place, but they should have known that the question should be about *who* could offer such provision. The Canaanite mom knew the answer. She knew that if you need breadcrumbs, you go to Jesus.

You see, when Jesus is involved, breadcrumbs are enough—enough to meet your needs, with leftovers enough to meet the needs of those you serve.

◆ ◆ ◆

Let's check back in on our Sinners Storyline.

THE SINNERS STORYLINE OF SCRIPTURE

Character	Why were they considered sinful?	How did they act in faith?
the disciple named Matthew (Matthew 9)	Matthew was a tax collector, and tax collectors were some of the most hated people in Jesus' day because they worked for the Romans and often stole money.	Matthew left his tollbooth behind to follow Jesus.
a Roman centurion (Luke 7)	The Roman centurion represented both the Romans, who were in a political and religious tug-of-war with the Jews, and the military, which was enforcing oppression of the Jews.	The Roman centurion advocated for his sick servant.
a sinful woman (Luke 7)	We don't know anything about her life or why she was considered sinful, but the Bible says that this was her reputation.	The sinful woman anointed Jesus' feet with an alabaster jar of perfume in a generous act of devotion.
a Canaanite mom (Matthew 15)	The Canaanites were known as the people group occupying the Promised Land before the Israelites.	The Canaanite mom begged Jesus to heal her demon-possessed daughter.
the Samaritan woman at the well (John 4)	The Samaritans were hated by the Jews for religious and ethnic animosity. They were considered half-breeds and sinful for their rejection of the Jerusalem Temple.	The Samaritan woman at the well believed Jesus was the Savior of the world and proclaimed it to her city.

What did Jesus say to them?	Who are they compared to in their story?	What was the outcome of their faith?
"Follow me."	Matthew and his friends are contrasted with the unrepentant Pharisees.	Jesus welcomed Matthew into his inner circle of disciples, healing him from feeling hated.
"I have not found so great a faith even in Israel."	The Roman centurion is contrasted with the passive crowd following Jesus.	Jesus healed the Roman centurion's sick servant.
"Your faith has saved you. Go in peace."	The sinful woman's love is contrasted with Simon the Pharisee's stingy hosting.	Jesus forgave the woman's sins, healing her soul.
"Woman, your faith is great. Let it be done for you as you want."	The Canaanite mom is contrasted with the disciples.	Jesus healed the woman's daughter.
"I, the one speaking to you, am he."	The Samaritan woman at the well is contrasted with Nicodemus the Pharisee in John 3.	Jesus met the woman's needs and changed—or healed—her story.

1. What about the Canaanite mom's story resonates with you most?

2. What did you learn about God's character in this lesson?

3. How should these truths shape your faith community and change you?

PART 4

RESPONDING

The purpose of Bible study is to help you become more Christlike; that's why part 4 will include journaling space for your reflection on and responses to the content and a blank checklist for actionable next steps. You'll be able to process what you're learning so that you can live out the concepts and pursue Christlikeness. Part 4 will enable you to answer the questions *What truths is this passage teaching?* and *How do I apply this to my life?*

THE CANAANITE MOM JOINS a prestigious list of women in the Bible who just wouldn't let something go—and whose protests were considered righteous acts of faith. She takes her place alongside

- Hannah, who petitioned God with such desperation the priest thought she was drunk (1 Samuel 1);
- Rizpah, the mother who relentlessly pursued dignity for her dead sons and got it (2 Samuel 21:10-14); and
- the persistent widow in Jesus' parable who was unrelenting in seeking justice (Luke 18:1-8).

All these amazing women believed that if they petitioned God for their deepest needs, he would act—and so should we. They could have chosen self-reliance or passivity, but instead they acted faithfully, entrusting themselves and those they loved to God.

Here are a few ways you and I could let the Canaanite mom's story change us.

1. ASK JESUS FOR HELP REGARDLESS OF YOUR STATUS.

The disciples tried to send the Canaanite mom away. They were completely unaffected by her pain. If anything, she was in their way, a nuisance to dispose of. She lacked the status that they believed made her worth caring about.

Here's the beauty of the gospel: Jesus does not submit to ancient or modern hierarchies of status. Jesus' compassion is for everyone. Don't let your perceived high or low status keep you from asking Jesus for help. We might give status a lot of merit, valuing others for their wealth, influence, or power. But Jesus' economy runs on grace.

2. ASK JESUS FOR HELP REGARDLESS OF YOUR SITUATION.

None of us want to air our dirty laundry. The struggles we face might feel too risky to share, too off-the-wall to believe, or just too embarrassing. Plus, what if people respond to our helplessness dismissively, like the disciples did? What if it feels like God is going to be silent on the matter forever?

Choose to ask Jesus for help regardless of your situation. The Canaanite mom showed that no matter what we are going through, no matter how messy or shameful it is, we will find an audience with Jesus. He won't send us away without what we need to survive the day. And don't worry about what you are going to say to Jesus when you ask for help. The Bible says that the Holy Spirit intercedes for us even when our requests can't be put into words (Romans 8:26).

3. ASK JESUS FOR HELP REGARDLESS OF THE SILENCE.

One of the most painful parts of being a Christian is experiencing the silence of God. Some call it a dark night of the soul. The agony of feeling as though God has turned away is real and traumatic.

You are not crazy if you feel as though God is taking a nap during your most painful moments. I believe this is part of being human, the reality of living between Jesus' resurrection and his return. Things are not as they are supposed to be.

But even in the silence, God is near. He cares. He hasn't forgotten you. He is not ignoring you to be cruel. God is love and can't be anything else.

I wish I had more concrete answers for you about why God sometimes seems silent when we are crying out for his help. We could go existential and talk about free will and how the world is broken. We could wrestle with some Scriptures in which Bible authors experience dark nights of the soul. But what I need most—and what you might need most—is a reminder that God's silence doesn't have to prevent us from continuing to ask him to meet our needs. Hannah didn't stop asking, Rizpah didn't stop protesting, the persistent widow didn't stop asking. And the Canaanite mom just kept on despite Jesus' momentary silence. Don't let the silence of God fool you. He's listening.

Use this journaling space to process what you are learning.

Ask yourself how these truths impact your relationship with God and with others.

What is the Holy Spirit bringing to your mind as actionable next steps in your faith journey?

- ◆
- ◆
- ◆

ANNOUNCING JESUS AS YOUR SAVIOR AND THE SAVIOR OF THE WORLD

THE SAMARITAN WOMAN:
THE FAITH OF THE WOMAN AT THE WELL

SCRIPTURE: JOHN 4

PART 1

CONTEXT

Before you begin your study, we will start with the context of the story we are about to read together: the setting, both cultural and historical; the people involved; and where our passage fits in the larger setting of Scripture. All these things help us make sense of what we're reading. Understanding the context of a Bible story is fundamental to reading Scripture well. Getting your bearings before you read will enable you to answer the question *What am I about to read?*

THE BIBLE IS BRIMMING WITH revolutionary female figures making a difference for God. God not only included these God-fearing women in his inspired Word, but he also seems to position them as standout characters in their stories. And it seems as though many of these women used by God were simply those willing to go first. Or "go messy early," as my friend Jenn would say. None of them had it all together; they were as broken as you and me. But they were willing to proclaim God's truth, even though they did so imperfectly.

- *Miriam*: the first worship leader for the nation of Israel
- *Deborah*: the first person to hold the offices of prophetess and judge and the only exemplary judge of the nation of Israel
- *Mary of Nazareth*: Jesus' mother and first disciple
- *Mary of Bethany*: the first female seminary student

- *Mary Magdalene*: the first gospel preacher
- *Lydia*: the first European Christian and the first church planter in Europe
- *Phoebe*: the first person to read and explain the book of Romans

In each story and situation, the Lord emphasizes his heart for women: They are indispensable.

The woman at the well in John 4 was also the first to do something for God: She's the first evangelist mentioned in John's Gospel. And while that might sound a bit intimidating and awe-inspiring, her evangelistic message was nothing of the sort. It was simple, short, incomplete, and imperfect. And yet it started revival in her city.

The woman at the well is nameless in her story. You see, John didn't want us to know her name. He wanted us to focus on her gender, her ethnicity, and her religion: She was a woman, and she was a Samaritan.

Jews and Samaritans were in a polarizing theological disagreement when Jesus met the woman at the well. Jews viewed Samaritans as half-breeds and ritually unclean. They hated each other because they disagreed on where to worship God. Jews believed the Temple belonged in Jerusalem, and Samaritans believed the Temple belonged on Mount Gerizim.

Samaria was the capital of the northern kingdom of Israel in the Old Testament and comes up several times in the Scriptures:

- *Isaiah 28*: The prophet Isaiah chastised and condemned the Samaritans for being drunkards. Isaiah painted a picture of the priests and prophets—the people supposed to be the most devoted to God—as stumbling around inebriated. Lest we think this sounds like a big frat party, Isaiah described all the Samaritan tables as covered in vomit. The putrid smell of the vomit was a signal you were close to Samaria.

- *Amos 3*: The prophet Amos described Samaria as full of "great turmoil," defined by "acts of oppression" and filled with people "incapable of doing right" (Amos 3:9-10).

Jews and Samaritans avoided one another like the plague, which makes Jesus' arrival in Samaria all the more curious. Most devout Jews would go out of their way to avoid Samaria, but John insists that Jesus "had" to go there (John 4:4). Jesus intended to travel there, knowing the assignment that waited at the end of the journey: sharing the gospel with the woman at the well. This encounter changed the course of Samaria's part in the story of Scripture:

- *Acts 1*: In the New Testament, Samaria would become a gateway to the gospel's spread across the world. Jesus said that after his followers received the Holy Spirit, they would be his "witnesses in Jerusalem, in all Judea and Samaria, and to the ends of the earth" (Acts 1:8). For Christianity to spread, it would have to go through Samaria.

What you are about to read is a story about a woman who was likely viewed as a sinner because of her past relationships, her current relationship status, her ethnicity, *and* her religion. And yet, despite every cultural and societal way she didn't measure up, she was the first outside the Temple to proclaim Jesus as the Savior of the world.

What you will see is that God wants to commission anyone, no matter how unlikely or broken, to tell the world who he is. This is good news for those of us—myself included—who feel like our attempts to share our faith are pitiful and inadequate. Neither our pasts nor our struggles prevent God from using us to bring revival to our cities when we are willing to share what we have: our broken, doubt-filled testimonies of the One who knows everything we've ever done.

1. **PERSONAL CONTEXT: What is going on in your life right now that might impact how you understand this Bible character?**

2. **SPIRITUAL CONTEXT: If you've never studied this Bible story before, what piques your curiosity? If you've studied this passage before, what impressions and insights do you recall?**

SEEING

Seeing the text is vital if we want the heart of the Scripture passage to sink in. We read slowly and intentionally through the text with the context in mind. As we practice close, thoughtful reading of Scripture, we pick up on phrases, implications, and meanings we might otherwise have missed. Part 2 includes close Scripture reading and observation questions to empower you to answer the question *What is the story saying?*

1. **Read John 4:1-30, 39-42 and draw a bubble around everything the Samaritan woman says to Jesus and to others.**

4 When Jesus learned that the Pharisees had heard he was making and baptizing more disciples than John [2] (though Jesus himself was not baptizing, but his disciples were), [3] he left Judea and went again to Galilee. [4] He had to travel through Samaria; [5] so he came to a town of Samaria called Sychar near the property that Jacob had given his son Joseph. [6] Jacob's well was there, and Jesus, worn out from his journey, sat down at the well. It was about noon.

[7] A woman of Samaria came to draw water.

"Give me a drink," Jesus said to her, [8] because his disciples had gone into town to buy food.

⁹ "How is it that you, a Jew, ask for a drink from me, a Samaritan woman?" she asked him. For Jews do not associate with Samaritans.

¹⁰ Jesus answered, "If you knew the gift of God, and who is saying to you, 'Give me a drink,' you would ask him, and he would give you living water."

¹¹ "Sir," said the woman, "you don't even have a bucket, and the well is deep. So where do you get this 'living water'? ¹² You aren't greater than our father Jacob, are you? He gave us the well and drank from it himself, as did his sons and livestock."

¹³ Jesus said, "Everyone who drinks from this water will get thirsty again. ¹⁴ But whoever drinks from the water that I will give him will never get thirsty again. In fact, the water I will give him will become a well of water springing up in him for eternal life."

¹⁵ "Sir," the woman said to him, "give me this water so that I won't get thirsty and come here to draw water."

¹⁶ "Go call your husband," he told her, "and come back here."

¹⁷ "I don't have a husband," she answered.

"You have correctly said, 'I don't have a husband,'" Jesus said. ¹⁸ "For you've had five husbands, and the man you now have is not your husband. What you have said is true."

¹⁹ "Sir," the woman replied, "I see that you are a prophet. ²⁰ Our ancestors worshiped on this mountain, but you Jews say that the place to worship is in Jerusalem."

²¹ Jesus told her, "Believe me, woman, an hour is coming when you will worship the Father neither on this mountain nor in Jerusalem. ²² You Samaritans worship what you do not know. We worship what we do know, because salvation is from the Jews. ²³ But an hour is coming, and is now here, when the true worshipers will worship the Father in Spirit and in truth. Yes, the Father wants such people to worship him. ²⁴ God is spirit, and those who worship him must worship in Spirit and in truth."

²⁵ The woman said to him, "I know that the Messiah is coming" (who is called Christ). "When he comes, he will explain everything to us."

²⁶ Jesus told her, "I, the one speaking to you, am he."

²⁷ Just then his disciples arrived, and they were amazed that he was talking with a woman. Yet no one said, "What do you want?" or "Why are you talking with her?"

²⁸ Then the woman left her water jar, went into town, and told the people, ²⁹ "Come, see a man who told me everything I ever did. Could this be the Messiah?" ³⁰ They left the town and made their way to him. . . .

³⁹ Now many Samaritans from that town believed in him because of what the woman said when she testified, "He told me everything I ever did." ⁴⁰ So when the Samaritans came to him, they asked him to stay with them, and he stayed there two days. ⁴¹ Many more believed because of what he said. ⁴² And they told the woman, "We no longer believe because of what you said, since we have heard for ourselves and know that this really is the Savior of the world."

JOHN 4:1-30, 39-42

2. **What geographical details does John give us about Jesus' journey to the woman at the well in John 4:4-5?**

- ◆
- ◆
- ◆

John writes that Jesus "had" to travel through Samaria—but Jesus doesn't *have* to do anything. He is the King of the universe. He is not without agency; no one was forcing him to go to Samaria. Jesus made a deliberate choice to go to Samaria so that he would encounter the woman at the well. Or to put it another way, Jesus had to go to Samaria to have a sacred conversation with a Samaritan woman. Jesus' love for you, for me, for the Samaritan woman, compels him to meet us where we are.[1]

3. **John tells us that Jesus got tired and sat down next to Jacob's well. In what ways might Jesus' posture have created a more welcoming environment for the woman at the well?**

   ◆

   ◆

   ◆

4. **Write out John 4:9 below.**

   "

   "

The woman at the well articulated the absurdity of the situation: a Jewish man talking alone with a divorced Samaritan woman. Jesus, though, was unfazed. He had a purpose in this conversation, and he would not be deterred.

5. **After Jesus explained that he is Living Water and that Living Water was exactly what the woman at the well needed, what did she do with this new information?**
   ☐ She laughed at Jesus.
   ☐ She rolled her eyes.
   ☐ She disagreed with Jesus.
   ☐ She accepted his words as true and asked for a drink of Living Water.
   ☐ She tried to change the subject.

Jesus knew the Samaritan woman's deepest need and met it with his presence. She was thirsty—not for water but for God's presence in her life. This is the

Notice too that Jesus is never said to drink the water the woman could have given him. The request for water simply serves as the occasion for the dialogue on religion in which Jesus will offer the woman something far more valuable than ordinary water.[2]

Ben Witherington III, *John's Wisdom*

longing under all her longings and beneath all ours. Parched for truth and craving security, she didn't need another man in her life; she needed Jesus, the One who meets all our needs.

Do you believe this about Jesus? You probably have pressing needs in this season of your life. You might even feel desperate to meet those needs. Ultimately, Jesus is the only person who can give you what you truly need.

Once the Samaritan woman recognized that Jesus was telling the truth and asked him for help, Jesus turned his attention to all the tender places in her story.

6. **What did Jesus ask the woman at the well to do once she was willing to receive his help? Write out Jesus' words in John 4:16.**

66

99

Jesus brought up her pain and suffering not to cause more pain or bring shame but because he is a compassionate Savior who wants to address all the hardships caused by unmet needs.

7. What do the Scriptures tell us about this woman's life? Check only the options that are clear from the text.

☐ She was a prostitute.

☐ She was an adulterous woman.

☐ She'd been married five times, and the man she was living with was not her husband.

☐ She'd been divorced several times.

We tend to make assumptions about the woman at the well. I used to imagine her as a scantily dressed, salty-mouthed temptress who lured men into her bed and divorced them as soon as she got bored. I pictured a conversation between Jesus and a prostitute, imagining Jesus calling her out for her sins and shaming her for her unchaste lifestyle choices. When the woman at the well agreed with Jesus that she'd had five husbands and the one she was with was not her husband, I got in my head that she was confessing to sexual immorality, had treated marriage flippantly, and was cohabiting for pleasure. Time and time again, I've read in the Bible examples of Jesus offering compassion and tenderness to sinners—but for this one woman, I'd always envisioned Jesus wagging his pointer finger in her face.

But I eventually realized that the Bible doesn't offer any evidence for this perspective. That's when I turned to some historical context. Could that help explain five marriages and a live-in boyfriend?

Based on some Bible scholarship, I'd like to suggest that the woman at the well was desperate to survive in a time when women were dependent on a man's provision and protection. To understand her predicament, let's look at some realities of marriage in the ancient world:

- "Most people in the ancient world got married—women often in their teens, men in their late twenties."[3]

- "If the woman at the well had been married five times and was on her sixth relationship, she must have been advanced in age, something that created even more vulnerability for women, since they were valued only as much as they were able to bear children."[4]

♦ "Given the high death rate, people were often widowed and then remarried, perhaps two or three times."[5]

♦ "It's unlikely that she was divorced five times, each time for committing adultery. No man would dare marry a convicted adulteress with neither fortune nor fame. That she was a serial divorcée is also unlikely. She would have needed the repeated help of a male advocate to do so."[6]

♦ "It is more likely that her five marriages and current arrangement were the result of unfortunate events that took the lives of several of her husbands."[7]

♦ "Having a man to provide for her may have been her only means of survival in a cultural system that made no provision for independent women."[8]

The Samaritan woman is not presented in the Bible as a cheater but as a woman who'd suffered more than most. The man she was living with likely took pity on her old age and agreed to take her on as a second wife or concubine to make sure her physical needs were met.

Based on our knowledge of the social and cultural values of first-century Palestine, why would it be unnatural to surmise that this woman is deserving of our sympathy rather than our opprobrium? In a society that granted to women essentially no social or legal standing apart from a responsible man—father, husband, brother or son—she can legitimately be considered a marginalized figure, subject to economic, social and legal exploitation.[9]

Janeth Norfleete Day, "The Woman at the Well"

The woman at the well had been married five times and was living with some-one who was not her husband . . . *to survive.*

8. **What are you surviving? Is there something in your life that is challenging your faith or keeping you up at night? Describe how this hardship is impacting the different areas of your life.**

What if Jesus' statements about the Samaritan woman's love life were not judgments but an acknowledgment of her life as a victim of a system that depersonalized her? What if Jesus was expressing his compassion and concern for the suffering she'd endured and the hardships she'd experienced?

Is it possible that when Jesus said, "Go call your husband" (John 4:16), she understood his meaning to be *I know how hard life has been for you*? When she answered that she was not married, is it possible that this was another way of saying, *This was the only way I could survive*? When Jesus said, "You've had five husbands, and the man you now have is not your husband" (John 4:18), do you think she understood his meaning to be *I see all your pain*?

Whatever you are going through, I want to remind you that Jesus cares deeply about your pain. He knows your story and he knows my story, and he loves us anyway. I know this because of how he cared for the woman at the well.

PART 3

UNDERSTANDING

Now that we've finished a close reading of the Scriptures, we're going to spend some time on interpretation: doing our best to understand what God was saying to the original audience and what he's teaching us through the process. But to do so, we need to learn his ways and consider how God's Word would have been understood by the original audience before applying the same truths to our own lives. "Scripture interpretation" may sound a little stuffy, but understanding what God means to communicate to us in the Bible is crucial to enjoying a close relationship with Jesus. Part 3 will enable you to answer the question *What does it mean?*

WHAT HAPPENS NEXT IN the Samaritan woman's story is usually interpreted as her attempt to change the subject. But I'm not convinced she was trying to deflect attention from her past. I think maybe for the first time in her whole life, she'd met a man who could give her everything she needed to survive—including truth about the right way to worship God.

1. Write out what the Samaritan woman says to Jesus in John 4:19-20.

"

"

2. Why do you think the woman at the well brought up this question to Jesus?

☐ Her question was a diversion tactic.

☐ Her question was sincere.

☐ I don't know why she asked this question.

When religious practice takes place in a temple and the only way to be in a relationship with God is to be in the Temple, religious people care about the Temple's access and location. The Samaritan woman asked the most important theological question of her day: *Where can I worship God?*

As Christ followers, you and I can worship God in any location—inside a church building, at home, or in our cars. Our bodies have become God's temple through the indwelling presence of the Holy Spirit (1 Corinthians 3:16). This was not the case for God-fearing people in the Old Testament and the Gospels, such as the Samaritan woman. She had to worship in the Temple. The difficulty she faced was trying to figure out which temple was the true Temple because both the Jews and the Samaritans laid claim to their temple being the real one. As you can imagine, part of the animosity between Jews and Samaritans was this theological disagreement about the location of the true Temple. Additionally, both groups of people forbade the other to access the inner temple courts because of their ethnicity. Jews treated Samaritans like unwelcome outsiders, and Samaritans did the same with Jews.

The Samaritans believed that Mount Gerizim was the holy place for sacrifice and that Moses was the Messiah, whereas Jews believed Jerusalem was the holy place for sacrifice and that a Messiah would come after Moses. That's why the Samaritan woman asked Jesus where to worship God. He'd just proved he was a prophet, and a prophet could answer the question that went directly to the heart of her relationship with God.

Jesus did not rebuke her for trying to skirt the subject; he answered her question. Maybe you have some burning question in mind for God. Ask him to reveal the truth to you through his Word and through the guidance of the Holy Spirit. If the Samaritan woman's story shows us anything, it's that Jesus welcomes hard questions about our faith—and he answers, too.

Neither her gender, her ethnicity, nor her religious commitments or practices are a barrier to Jesus' gracious gift to her. Neither should they be a barrier to the mission of Jesus' disciples to her and her townspeople, as the narrative will shortly make clear.[10]

Marianne Meye Thompson, *John: A Commentary*

3. **Summarize Jesus' answer to the woman at the well (John 4:21-24) in your own words below.**

Jesus explained that *how*, not *where*, someone approached God would be the litmus test for true faith: "True worshipers will worship the Father in Spirit and in truth" (John 4:23).

As difficult as it may have been to accept Jesus' words, which went against every tradition she knew, the woman at the well seemed to take them in with readiness. Emboldened by all the truth Jesus had entrusted to her, she brought the good news of a new way of worship to the rest of her community. And they believed her!

You know what she said in response to Jesus' Bible lesson? She said she *knew* that the Messiah was coming and that when he did, he would explain everything. Whether the Messiah was going to be Moses or someone else, the Samaritans believed that he would explain everything—which is how the woman at the well recognized Jesus as the Messiah.

An important part of understanding the meaning of a Bible passage is getting a sense of its place in the broader storyline of Scripture. When we make connections between different parts of the Bible, we get a glimpse of the unity and cohesion of the Scriptures.

An important note: If sexual violence toward women is a trigger for you, you might want to pick back up in part 4 of this lesson. But you should know before you skip that God is not okay with the way you were abused. You are so loved.

Jesus met the Samaritan woman at a well in Sychar, a place that shows up all over the Old Testament under a different name: Shechem. Many tragic events took place in Sychar/Shechem, one being the rape of Dinah in Genesis 34.

When we compare Dinah's experience in Sychar/Shechem with the woman at the well's experience, we see Jesus' insistence on redeeming a geographical location with so much history. The places in our lives that are, metaphorically speaking, do-not-enter zones are where Jesus rushes in to show his compassion.

Dinah (Genesis 34)	The Woman at the Well (John 4)
Dinah is the first daughter in the Bible whose name is mentioned at birth.	The woman at the well is nameless in the text. But Jesus knew her name.
Shechem was the prince of a region that later became known by his name, and he brought terror to those around him.	Jesus is the Prince of Peace; his presence makes us feel safe.
Jacob was silent about Dinah's rape. He was likely motivated to keep his power—the rapist's father owned the land Jacob lived on.	Jesus initiated a conversation with the woman at the well even though he already knew her story. Jesus is always giving away his power.
Dinah's voice is never heard in Genesis 34.	Jesus invited the woman at the well to tell her story from her point of view, and he listened. Jesus welcomed her voice! This is one of the longest continuous narratives in the New Testament.
The story ends with mass genocide.	The story ends with the town being saved.
Dinah's story begins ominously and casually—she wanted to see her friends.	Jesus "had" to go to Samaria—he had divine determination to see one person.
Dinah was at the mercy of Shechem's lust, and he failed to protect her honor. He used her as an object of his infatuation.	The woman was at the mercy of Jesus' love, and he protected her and released her to go and tell her testimony.
Shechem had predatorial behavior, hunting his victim. We get the sense that we need to hide from him.	Jesus sat down, made himself approachable, and welcomed an unclean woman into his presence to save her.
Jacob's failures as a patriarch left women vulnerable.	Jesus is "greater than our father Jacob" (John 4:12).

Jacob's failures as a patriarch left Dinah vulnerable, but Jesus is better than Jacob. In fact, this was one of the questions the Samaritan woman asked of Jesus: "You aren't greater than our father Jacob, are you?" (John 4:12). The answer is yes. Jesus *is* greater.

◆　◆　◆

Let's check back in on our Sinners Storyline.

THE SINNERS STORYLINE OF SCRIPTURE

Character	Why were they considered sinful?	How did they act in faith?
the disciple named Matthew (Matthew 9)	Matthew was a tax collector, and tax collectors were some of the most hated people in Jesus' day because they worked for the Romans and often stole money.	Matthew left his tollbooth behind to follow Jesus.
a Roman centurion (Luke 7)	The Roman centurion repre-sented both the Romans, who were in a political and religious tug-of-war with the Jews, and the military, which was enforc-ing oppression of the Jews.	The Roman centurion advocated for his sick servant.
a sinful woman (Luke 7)	We don't know anything about her life or why she was considered sinful, but the Bible says that this was her reputation.	The sinful woman anointed Jesus' feet with an alabaster jar of perfume in a generous act of devotion.
a Canaanite mom (Matthew 15)	The Canaanites were known as the people group occupy-ing the Promised Land before the Israelites.	The Canaanite mom begged Jesus to heal her demon-possessed daughter.
the Samaritan woman at the well (John 4)	The Samaritans were hated by the Jews for religious and ethnic animosity. They were considered half-breeds and sinful for their rejection of the Jerusalem Temple.	The Samaritan woman at the well believed Jesus was the Savior of the world and proclaimed it to her city.

What did Jesus say to them?	Who are they compared to in their story?	What was the outcome of their faith?
"Follow me."	Matthew and his friends are contrasted with the unrepentant Pharisees.	Jesus welcomed Matthew into his inner circle of disciples, healing him from feeling hated.
"I have not found so great a faith even in Israel."	The Roman centurion is contrasted with the passive crowd following Jesus.	Jesus healed the Roman centurion's sick servant.
"Your faith has saved you. Go in peace."	The sinful woman's love is contrasted with Simon the Pharisee's stingy hosting.	Jesus forgave the woman's sins, healing her soul.
"Woman, your faith is great. Let it be done for you as you want."	The Canaanite mom is contrasted with the disciples.	Jesus healed the woman's daughter.
"I, the one speaking to you, am he."	The Samaritan woman at the well is contrasted with Nicodemus the Pharisee in John 3.	Jesus met the woman's needs and changed—or healed—her story.

1. What about the Samaritan woman's story resonates with you most?

2. What did you learn about God's character in this lesson?

3. How should these truths shape your faith community and change you?

RESPONDING

The purpose of Bible study is to help you become more Christlike; that's why part 4 will include journaling space for your reflection on and responses to the content and a blank checklist for actionable next steps. You'll be able to process what you're learning so that you can live out the concepts and pursue Christlikeness. Part 4 will enable you to answer the questions *What truths is this passage teaching?* and *How do I apply this to my life?*

BEFORE HER CONVERSION, the woman at the well would have been considered an unlikely convert. She was the wrong gender: Not only were women considered second-class citizens, but if a man were even simply near a woman alone, he risked being stigmatized as a sinner. She was in the wrong relationship: Not only had she lost or been divorced from multiple husbands, but she was living as a concubine to survive. And she was the wrong ethnicity: Her Jewish neighbors hated her and her people because of their religious differences. In sum, she was all wrong.

It's not lost on me that many reading this now may feel the same way. You feel like everything about you is wrong. The mirror shouts a litany of grievances and condemnations at you. You feel like you're too much or not enough, too loud or too quiet. Or perhaps the Samaritan woman's story has unearthed some hurts buried deep in your soul. Surviving this life has forced you to make some hard choices and subjected you to systems that have marginalized you.

Whatever our struggle, we are not alone. We have scriptural examples of people who were "all wrong"—like the woman at the well—who can reframe our view of ourselves and of others. And, of course, we have something much greater: Jesus.

Our Savior will cross any boundary necessary to find us, restore us, teach us truth, and commission us to share that truth with others. As we internalize the Samaritan woman's story, I'm hoping you will consider these three exhortations.

1. ASK JESUS YOUR QUESTIONS.

One of my friends recently admitted that she was scared to seek out truth. She knew it could be paradigm shifting. You might resonate with her fear. But here's the thing about truth: It sets us free (John 8:32). Our God welcomes our questions, takes the time to answer them, and entrusts us with truth so that we can live freed. If anyone is safe enough for you to interrogate, it is Jesus. In his life, death, and resurrection, he proved just how willing he is to be questioned and how much he would suffer to liberate us from the penalty and power of sin.

So ask Jesus your burning questions. Do a word study in the Scriptures. Pull out your trusted concordance. Dig deep. You may not find all the answers you want, but Jesus will give you enough to meet your needs. And you won't find him too evasive or confusing. You might find that he is mysterious and that some of his ways are beyond comprehension, but ask anyway. Because I promise: You'll also find him to be good.

2. ACCEPT JESUS' ANSWERS.

For all the unanswered questions we may have, the Bible has sufficient answers to show us the way, the truth, and the life Jesus intends us to live. Whom Jesus talks to, the way he talks to them, what he says, when he chooses to say it—these are the things we should process as answers to our deepest questions. There is plenty we won't know this side of heaven, but we have more than enough of Jesus' answers in the Bible to anchor our faith for the rest of our lives.

I want to encourage you not to get distracted or bogged down by the mysteries of God. Appreciate them, and then grab hold of the answers Jesus does provide. He has provided everything we need for life and godliness (2 Peter 1:3). The question remains: When Jesus answers us, will we accept his truth? The challenge before us is not only to bring our questions to Jesus but to be willing and humble enough to receive his answers as gospel truth.

3. ANNOUNCE JESUS AS THE SAVIOR OF THE WORLD.

The woman at the well dropped her water jug and started running back to her city to share the good news. Her testimony wasn't practiced or refined. She didn't script out her story or take time to overthink how to word her experience. She dropped what she was doing and took off with the speed of the gospel.

And what was this amazing sermon that converted droves of people in her city and started a revival? What message solidified the woman's role as the first evangelist in the Bible? "Come, see a man who told me everything I ever did. Could this be the Messiah?" (John 4:29).

Does that sound like an eloquent, five-point gospel presentation to you? To me, it sounds like a broken woman undone by Jesus' love and sharing with others what she was still processing herself: This man, this Jesus, knew everything about her and loved her anyway. Could he be the long-promised Messiah?

Her testimony carried the assurance of someone who'd been changed forever, so confident in her relationship with Jesus that she didn't hesitate to bravely announce it to the people in her world. But her words also surfaced unanswered questions for those who heard, and only Jesus could answer. So the people in her town went to Jesus themselves.

We don't need to overcomplicate evangelism. Share what Jesus has done and continues to do in your life, and point people to him. He is ready to answer their questions.

Use this journaling space to process what you are learning.

Ask yourself how these truths impact your relationship with God and with others.

What is the Holy Spirit bringing to your mind as actionable next steps in your faith journey?

- ◆
- ◆
- ◆

As You Go

YOU DID IT. You studied five Bible stories in which "sinful" people exhibited great faith in Christ.

- Although Matthew was a tax collector, a man hated by his fellow Jews and considered sinful for his profession of extortion, he repented, believed in Jesus, and showed his faith by leaving his security behind.

- Although the Roman centurion was considered sinful by the Jews for being in the Roman army, and although we know his slave ownership was sinful, faith in Christ compelled him to advocate for and use all his tangible and intangible resources on behalf of his sick servant.

- Although the woman with the alabaster jar is identified only by the title *sinner*, she offered her best to Christ, anointing his feet with her most precious asset.

THE SINNERS STORYLINE OF SCRIPTURE

Character	Why were they considered sinful?	How did they act in faith?
the disciple named Matthew (Matthew 9)	Matthew was a tax collector, and tax collectors were some of the most hated people in Jesus' day because they worked for the Romans and often stole money.	Matthew left his tollbooth behind to follow Jesus.
a Roman centurion (Luke 7)	The Roman centurion represented both the Romans, who were in a political and religious tug-of-war with the Jews, and the military, which was enforcing oppression of the Jews.	The Roman centurion advocated for his sick servant.
a sinful woman (Luke 7)	We don't know anything about her life or why she was considered sinful, but the Bible says that this was her reputation.	The sinful woman anointed Jesus' feet with an alabaster jar of perfume in a generous act of devotion.
a Canaanite mom (Matthew 15)	The Canaanites were known as the people group occupying the Promised Land before the Israelites.	The Canaanite mom begged Jesus to heal her demon-possessed daughter.
the Samaritan woman at the well (John 4)	The Samaritans were hated by the Jews for religious and ethnic animosity. They were considered half-breeds and sinful for their rejection of the Jerusalem Temple.	The Samaritan woman at the well believed Jesus was the Savior of the world and proclaimed it to her city.

What did Jesus say to them?	Who are they compared to in their story?	What was the outcome of their faith?
"Follow me."	Matthew and his friends are contrasted with the unrepentant Pharisees.	Jesus welcomed Matthew into his inner circle of disciples, healing him from feeling hated.
"I have not found so great a faith even in Israel."	The Roman centurion is contrasted with the passive crowd following Jesus.	Jesus healed the Roman centurion's sick servant.
"Your faith has saved you. Go in peace."	The sinful woman's love is contrasted with Simon the Pharisee's stingy hosting.	Jesus forgave the woman's sins, healing her soul.
"Woman, your faith is great. Let it be done for you as you want."	The Canaanite mom is contrasted with the disciples.	Jesus healed the woman's daughter.
"I, the one speaking to you, am he."	The Samaritan woman at the well is contrasted with Nicodemus the Pharisee in John 3.	Jesus met the woman's needs and changed—or healed—her story.

- Although the Canaanite mom was considered sinful for being a part of a group of people who usually stood in the way of God's promises to his people, she acted with great faith and petitioned Jesus for her daughter's healing.

- Although the woman at the well was reviled by the Jews because she was a Samaritan, she believed Jesus was the Messiah and started a revival in her city.

What is your "although"? What label have you carried? How have you been made to feel disliked or hated? In what ways do you carry sin, shame, or struggles? God does not leave you there.

What God does with the archetype of the righteous sinner in the New Testament is show us that our struggles and failures are not barriers to relationship with him and participation in his Kingdom. These people seem disqualified from acting faithfully—yet still they choose to move toward Jesus. In their own ways, they humble themselves to believe that Jesus is their Savior. That he will be their True Security, their Lord, their Great Advocate, their Healer, and the Savior of the world.

I hope that this is the message you carry with you from the *Sinners* Bible study: that we need to humble ourselves, repent when necessary, and choose to act on our faith even when it will cost us a great deal. Jesus will meet us there. Sin, struggles, and shame cannot keep us from him. According to the Scriptures, Jesus' compassion for sinners like you and me knows no bounds. His tenderness sets us free.

PS: I've loved this journey with you, and I hope you join me again—this time, for the *Saints* study.

Each **Storyline Bible Study** is five lessons long and can be paired with its thematic partner for a seamless ten-week study. Complement the *Sinners* study with

SAINTS
ENJOYING A RELATIONSHIP WITH JESUS
WHEN YOU'RE DISILLUSIONED WITH RELIGION

In *Saints*, we will look at characters and themes that are cautionary tales for Christians and Christian leaders. None of us are above the actions described in the Bible, and all of us need the redemption and restoration of God.

LESSON ONE: Accepting Jesus' Words When They Challenge Your Worldview
Nicodemus: The Pharisee Who Is Disoriented by Jesus' Testimony
JOHN 3, 7, 19

LESSON TWO: Remaining Loyal to Jesus When You Are Tempted to Betray Him
Judas: The Disciple Who Sells Jesus Out
JOHN 6, 12, 13, 18

LESSON THREE: Using Your Influence for Good When It Doesn't Benefit You
Caiaphas: The High Priest Who Protects His Power
JOHN 11, 18; ACTS 4

LESSON FOUR: Identifying with Jesus When Your Reputation Is on the Line
Peter: The Disciple Who Denies Being Connected to Jesus
JOHN 18, 21

LESSON FIVE: Regaining Clarity When You're Blinded by Passion
Paul: The Pharisee Who Persecutes Christians
ACTS 8; 1 TIMOTHY 1

Learn more at thestorylineproject.com.

CP1904

Storyline Bible Studies

Each study follows people, places, or things throughout the Bible.
This approach allows you to see the cohesive storyline of Scripture
and appreciate the Bible as the literary masterpiece that it is.

**Access free resources to help you teach or
lead a small group at thestorylineproject.com.**

STORYLINE

CP1816

Acknowledgments

WITHOUT MY FAMILY'S SUPPORT, the **Storyline Bible Studies** would just be a dream. I'm exceedingly grateful for a family that prays and cheers for me when I step out to try something new. To my husband, Aaron, son, Caleb, and mom, Noemi: You three sacrificed the most to ensure that I had enough time and space to write. Thank you. And to all my extended family: I know an army of Armstrongs was praying and my family in Austin was cheering me on to the finish line. Thank you.

To my ministry partners at the Polished Network, Integrus Leadership, and Dallas Bible Church: Linking arms with you made this project possible. I love doing Kingdom work with you.

NavPress and Tyndale teams: Thank you for believing in me. You wholeheartedly embraced the concept, and you've made this project better in every way possible. Special thanks to David Zimmerman, my amazing editor Caitlyn Carlson, Elizabeth Schroll, Olivia Eldredge, David Geeslin, and the entire editorial and marketing teams.

Jana Burson: You were the catalyst. Thank you.

Teresa Swanstrom Anderson: Thank you for connecting me with Caitlyn. You'll forever go down in history as the person who made my dreams come true.

All my friends rallied to pray for this project when I was stressed about the deadlines. Thank you. We did it! Without your intercession, these wouldn't be complete. I want to give special thanks to Lee, Sarah, Amy, Ashton, Tiffany, and Jenn for holding up my arms to complete the studies.

Resources for Deeper Study

OLD TESTAMENT

Bearing God's Name: Why Sinai Still Matters by Carmen Joy Imes

The Epic of Eden: A Christian Entry into the Old Testament by Sandra L. Richter

NEW TESTAMENT

Echoes of Scripture in the Gospels by Richard B. Hays

The Gospels as Stories: A Narrative Approach to Matthew, Mark, Luke, and John by Jeannine K. Brown

BIBLE STUDY

Commentary on the New Testament Use of the Old Testament, eds. G. K. Beale and D. A. Carson

Dictionary of Biblical Imagery, eds. Leland Ryken, James C. Wilhoit, and Tremper Longman III

The Drama of Scripture: Finding Our Place in the Biblical Story by Craig G. Bartholomew and Michael W. Goheen

From Beginning to Forever: A Study of the Grand Narrative of Scripture by Elizabeth Woodson

How (Not) to Read the Bible: Making Sense of the Anti-Women, Anti-Science, Pro-Violence, Pro-Slavery and Other Crazy Sounding Parts of Scripture by Dan Kimball

How to Read the Bible as Literature . . . and Get More Out of It by Leland Ryken

Literarily: How Understanding Bible Genres Transforms Bible Study by Kristie Anyabwile

The Mission of God: Unlocking the Bible's Grand Narrative by Christopher J. H. Wright

"Reading Scripture as a Coherent Story" by Richard Bauckham, in *The Art of Reading Scripture*, eds. Ellen F. Davis and Richard B. Hays

Reading While Black: African American Biblical Interpretation as an Exercise in Hope by Esau McCaulley

Read the Bible for a Change: Understanding and Responding to God's Word by Ray Lubeck

Scripture as Communication: Introducing Biblical Hermeneutics by Jeannine K. Brown

What Is the Bible and How Do We Understand It? by Dennis R. Edwards

Words of Delight: A Literary Introduction to the Bible by Leland Ryken

About the Author

KAT ARMSTRONG was born in Houston, Texas, where the humidity ruins her Mexi-German curls. She is a powerful voice in our generation as a sought-after Bible teacher. She holds a master's degree from Dallas Theological Seminary and is the author of *No More Holding Back*, *The In-Between Place*, and the **Storyline Bible Studies**. In 2008, Kat cofounded the Polished Network to embolden working women in their faith and work. Kat is pursuing a doctorate of ministry in New Testament context at Northern Seminary and is a board member of the Polished Network. She and her husband, Aaron, have been married for twenty years; live in Dallas, Texas, with their son, Caleb; and attend Dallas Bible Church, where Aaron serves as the lead pastor.

KATARMSTRONG.COM   **THESTORYLINEPROJECT.COM**
@KATARMSTRONG1   **@THESTORYLINEPROJECT**

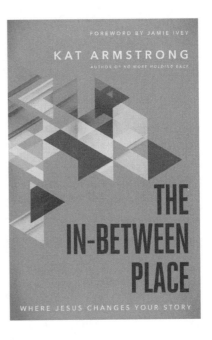

Make peace with your past.
Find hope in the present.
Step into your future.

W Publishing Group

An Imprint of Thomas Nelson

Available everywhere books are sold.

CP1818

Notes

INTRODUCTION
1. Michael F. Bird, "Sin, Sinner," in *Dictionary of Jesus and the Gospels*, 2nd ed., eds. Joel B. Green, Jeannine K. Brown, and Nicholas Perrin (Downers Grove, IL: IVP Academic, 2013), 863.
2. Bird, "Sin, Sinner," in *Dictionary of Jesus and the Gospels*, 863.

LESSON ONE | LEAVING YOUR SECURITY BEHIND TO FOLLOW JESUS
1. Jeffrey E. Miller, "Tax Collector," in *The Lexham Bible Dictionary*, eds. John D. Barry et al. (Bellingham, WA: Lexham Press, 2016).
2. Miller, "Tax Collector," in *The Lexham Bible Dictionary*.
3. Miller, "Tax Collector," in *The Lexham Bible Dictionary*.
4. Martin H. Manser, Alister E. McGrath, J. I. Packer, and Donald J. Wiseman, eds., "5576 tax collectors," in *The Complete Topical Guide to the Bible* (Grand Rapids, MI: Baker Books, 2017), 325.
5. Miller, "Taxation," in *The Lexham Bible Dictionary*.
6. Miller, "Taxation," in *The Lexham Bible Dictionary*.
7. Miller, "Taxation," in *The Lexham Bible Dictionary*.
8. Miller, "Taxation," in *The Lexham Bible Dictionary*.
9. Miller, "Taxation," in *The Lexham Bible Dictionary*.
10. Michael F. Bird, "Sin, Sinner," in *Dictionary of Jesus and the Gospels*, 2nd ed., eds. Joel B. Green, Jeannine K. Brown, and Nicholas Perrin (Downers Grove, IL: IVP Academic, 2013), 866.
11. Jeannine K. Brown and Kyle Roberts, *Matthew*, The Two Horizons New Testament Commentary (Grand Rapids, MI: Eerdmans, 2018), 94.
12. Bird, "Sin, Sinner," in *Dictionary of Jesus and the Gospels*, 867.

LESSON TWO | ADVOCATING FOR YOUR LOVED ONES WITH ALL YOU'VE GOT
1. Diane G. Chen, *Luke: A New Covenant Commentary*, New Covenant Commentary Series (Eugene, OR: Cascade Books, 2017), 94.

2. Chen, *Luke*, 92.

3. Takatemjen, "Luke," in *South Asia Bible Commentary: A One-Volume Commentary on the Whole Bible*, ed. Brian Wintle (Grand Rapids, MI: Zondervan, 2015), 1349.

LESSON THREE | OFFERING YOUR BEST TO GOD EVEN WHEN IT CAUSES A COMMOTION

1. Diane G. Chen, *Luke: A New Covenant Commentary*, New Covenant Commentary Series (Eugene, OR: Cascade Books, 2017), 105.

2. Amy-Jill Levine and Ben Witherington III, *The Gospel of Luke*, New Cambridge Bible Commentary (Cambridge: Cambridge University Press, 2018), 211.

3. Levine and Witherington III, *The Gospel of Luke*, 215.

4. Chen, *Luke*, 105.

5. Barbara E. Reid and Shelly Matthews, *Luke 1–9*, Wisdom Commentary vol. 43A (Collegeville, MN: Liturgical Press, 2021), 238.

6. Takatemjen, "Luke," in *South Asia Bible Commentary: A One-Volume Commentary on the Whole Bible*, ed. Brian Wintle (Grand Rapids, MI: Zondervan, 2015), 1350.

LESSON FOUR | PETITIONING JESUS FOR YOUR DEEPEST NEEDS

1. Barbara E. Reid, *The Gospel according to Matthew Part One: Matthew 1–16* (Collegeville, MN: Liturgical Press, 2019), 88.

2. Michael Joseph Brown, "Matthew," in *True to Our Native Land: An African American New Testament Commentary*, ed. Brian K. Blount (Minneapolis: Fortress Press, 2007), 106.

3. Jeannine K. Brown and Kyle Roberts, *Matthew*, The Two Horizons New Testament Commentary (Grand Rapids, MI: Eerdmans, 2018), 146.

LESSON FIVE | ANNOUNCING JESUS AS YOUR SAVIOR AND THE SAVIOR OF THE WORLD

1. Kat Armstrong, *The In-Between Place: Where Jesus Changes Your Story* (Nashville: W Publishing, 2021), 18.

2. Ben Witherington III, *John's Wisdom: A Commentary on the Fourth Gospel* (Louisville: Westminster John Knox, 1995), 120.

3. Lynn Cohick, "The 'Woman at the Well': Was the Samaritan Woman Really an Adulteress?" in *Vindicating the Vixens: Revisiting Sexualized, Vilified, and Marginalized Women of the Bible*, ed. Sandra Glahn (Grand Rapids, MI: Kregel Academic, 2017), 250.

4. Armstrong, *The In-Between Place*, 122.

5. Cohick, "The 'Woman at the Well,'" in *Vindicating the Vixens*, 250.

6. Cohick, "The 'Woman at the Well,'" in *Vindicating the Vixens*, 251.

7. Cohick, "The 'Woman at the Well,'" in *Vindicating the Vixens*, 251.

8. Janeth Norfleete Day, "The Woman at the Well: Interpretation of John 4:1-42 in Retrospect and Prospect" (PhD diss., Baylor University, 1999), 222.

9. Day, "The Woman at the Well," 219.

10. Marianne Meye Thompson, *John: A Commentary*, The New Testament Library (Louisville: Westminster John Knox, 2015), 99.